LIFE AS PRAYER
AND OTHER WRITINGS OF
EVELYN UNDERHILL

LIFE AS PRAYER
and Other Writings of
EVELYN UNDERHILL

originally published as

Collected Papers of Evelyn Underhill

Edited by Lucy Menzies

MOREHOUSE PUBLISHING
Harrisburg, PA

© 1946 Longman Group UK Limited. First published by Longmans, Green and Co., Ltd. as *Collected Papers of Evelyn Underhill*.

First American paperback edition published by

Morehouse Publishing

Editorial Office
871 Ethan Allen Highway
Suite 204
Ridgefield, CT 06877

Corporate Office
P.O. Box 1321
Harrisburg, PA 17105

Library of Congress Cataloging-in-Publication Data
Underhill, Evelyn, 1875-1941.
    [Selections. 1991]
    Life as prayer and other writings of Evelyn Underhill / edited by Lucy Menzies.—1st American pbk. ed.
        p.   cm.
    Reprint. Originally published: Collected papers of Evelyn Underhill. London: Longmans, Green, 1946.
    Contents: The degrees of prayer—Life as prayer—Worship—Thoughts on prayer and the divine immanence—The inside of life—What is mysticism?—The parish priest and the life of prayer—The teacher's vocation—The spiritual life of the teacher—Education and the spirit of worship.
    ISBN 0-8192-1576-7
    1. Mysticism.   2. Prayer—Christianity.
3. Teachers—Religious life.   I. Menzies, Lucy.   II. Title.
BV5085.U53   1991   91-18022
248—dc20   CIP

Printed in the United States of America
by
BSC LITHO
Harrisburg, PA

CONTENTS

Permission to reprint these papers has been generously given by the following:

The Council of the Guild of Health, *The Degrees of Prayer*, 1922.

Publications Department of the Church of Scotland, *Life as Prayer*, 1928.

Dr. A. W. Hastings, Editor, and T. & T. Clark, publishers of *The Expository Times*, *Thoughts on Prayer and the Divine Immanence*, 1931.

A. R. Mowbray & Co. Ltd., *Worship*, 1929; *The Inside of Life* (Broadcast, 1931); *What is Mysticism?* (1936); *The Parish Priest and the Life of Prayer* (1937).

The National Society, *The Teacher's Vocation*, 1927.

The Guild of the Epiphany, *The Spiritual Life of the Teacher* and *Worship*, 1934.

The Principal of Whitelands College, *Education and the Spirit of Worship*, 1937.

INTRODUCTION

BY the mercy of God, *Practical Mysticism* came into my hands at a time of great need. It was given to me at the first Christmas of the Great War, in 1914. I had been prepared for its message by many years of searching without finding and it spoke straight to the heart of my condition. It is not by popular choice (nor by her own) the best of Evelyn Underhill's books; but it is the one to which I owe more than to any other theological book I have ever read.

Books, like persons, are fortunate or unfortunate in the time at which their readers and themselves are introduced to each other. I was fortunate in the coincidence of the publication of *Practical Mysticism* with a peculiarly receptive frame of mind, partly due to my own phase of spiritual development, partly to the new complexion thrown on human experience by the outbreak of war. (We who are hardened by recent events can hardly realize how utterly shattering to all one's customary outlook and habit of thought was the cataclysmic irruption of arms in a world where it was almost taken for granted that war was as outmoded as duelling.)

I had previously read Evelyn Underhill's two longer books, *Mysticism* and *The Mystic Way*, and been greatly interested. But the intimate appeal of the smaller volume, with its characteristically homely illustrations, spoke to me as directly as the quiet voice of Thomas à Kempis spoke to Maggie Tulliver on the Lincolnshire Wolds. Evelyn Underhill threw open a door before which I had been standing all my life, longing to get through. She encouraged me to make the experiment which the previous guides of my university and theological college days (mainly of the Ritschlian school of thought) had said was beyond human capacity; and she assured me that direct and first-hand knowledge of God was not only desirable but possible. Many years before when Dr. Inge published his *Christian Mysticism* I had read it with avidity, thinking that perhaps in it I would find the Gospel after which I dimly groped; but the Oxford don (as he then was) seemed himself to speak with so much uncertainty and as a recorder of others' vision rather than as one possessing a vision of his own, that I gained from him no reassurance. I thought of his work when later in *The Essentials of Mysticism* I read Evelyn Underhill's remark, "For some time much attention has been given to the historical side of mysticism, and some—much less—to its practice . . . so that much of this literature seems to the reader to refer to some self-consistent and exclusive dream-world, and not to the achievement of universal truth."[1] In *Practical Mysticism* she "disentangled the facts from ancient formulæ used to express them" and made them pertinent and relevant to the life of to-day.

In his book, *Redeeming the Time*, Maritain makes some comments about Bergson. By changing the capital nouns *France* and *Bergson* to *Britain* and *Evelyn Underhill*, his words are an exact description of her achievement.

"Thirty years ago in France the word 'mysticism' stirred up all sorts of reactions of mistrust

[1] *Essentials of Mysticism*, p. 1.

and uneasiness. One could not hear it spoken without immediately being on one's guard against an eventual invasion of fanaticism and hysteria. . . . . Now we understand better and better that the more or less pathological counterfeits of the mystical life are doubtless numerous, but that the true mystics are the wisest of men and the best witnesses for the spirit. Bergson himself has had a great deal to do with the change."[1]

This, then, has been her life-work; for this she will be remembered. Because of her temperament and her acquired attainments she was uniquely qualified to render this inestimable service to her fellows. She herself was a mystic and not a mere "mystical philosopher." She has described the difference as equivalent to that which separates theology from revelation. The mystics' experience "provides the material, the substance, the actual experience upon which mystical philosophy cogitates, as the theologians cogitate upon the individual revelations which form the basis of faith." The mystics "must have 'lived the life'; submitted to the interior travail of the Mystic Way, not merely have reasoned about the mystical experience of others."[2] This she had done; she spoke out of the depth of her own experience. She was well aware of the danger of "mysticality" and the fatuousness of those who complacently remark, "I'm a bit of a mystic myself," and the snare of "browsing on mystical books." (See her Introduction to Malaval.) The point for us is that she was essentially modern with a mind acutely sensitive to the currents of contemporary thought, and

[1] Maritain, *Redeeming the Time*, p. 75.
[2] *Mysticism*, 1st edition, p. 98. (All quotations from *Mysticism* are from the 1st edition.)

capable of understanding the mental climate of her age. She possessed a nature very similar to that of Pascal (of whom however she was inclined to speak deprecatingly), at once rationalistic and sceptical and, still more, sensitively receptive of the frail and exiguous communications which pass to us from the supernatural world. More than most she was habitually aware that

Strange poignant dreams the soul invade—
News from beyond our stubborn ramparts blown . . .
    Those ramparts they are builded tall;
    But we a secret gate possess
    That opens in the outer wall
    What time its living latch we press:
A little emerald gate that sets us free
              Within eternity.[1]

Fastidious to a degree in style and use of words, she was equally so in her dealings with truth. She had a profound humility of mind which was ceaselessly prepared to revise its opinions and open its horizons for the incoming of larger views of reality. The essential characteristic of the Greek genius has recently been described as "an unshakable trust in reason, and a capacity for seeing, and even up to a point, of sympathizing with the view of an opponent."[2] Evelyn Underhill had a carefully reasoned-out view of the limitations of reason and an abnormally acute insight into the mind of others. Hers was the Greek nature sublimated and sanctified. She had the power of seeing, which, as Ruskin said, gives to its possessor the power of being an artist, a

[1] *Theophanies*, p. vi.
[2] Prof. J. A. K. Thomson, Introduction to Gilbert Murray's *Myths and Ethics*.

poet, a philosopher and a spiritual initiate. She was all these at once. She loved working with her hands and produced many lovely things. Her two volumes of poetry contain verse which is certain to be remembered when a great deal of what now passes under the name will be ridiculed or forgotten; and her prose, without self-conscious artifice, is exquisitely wrought to be an adequate vehicle for her thought. She is adept in selecting the right word. (What, for instance could be better than the unexpected adjective "eager" in describing the face of a primrose?) Passages of great dignity are found in the appropriate places (as in the magnificent closing pages of *Mysticism*), and the homeliest language and metaphor are used when she seeks to make her message clear. As a philosopher, her Platonic outlook was closely joined to that of the Pragmatist; and this may explain the delightful combination of style in her prose. She knew, as she said, that the mystic "is called to a life more active because more contemplative, than that of other men"; and her manner of writing makes it obvious that she always had this active life in view. Not only in her Retreat addresses but elsewhere, she will suddenly illustrate her point with a quite mundane metaphor, linking the extremest altitude of thought with the most prosaic duty of daily routine. This means, of course, that she had in a marked degree the divine gift of humour which the professionally religious person finds so disconcerting. She possessed this in common with other mystics. Of Abbot Chapman, whom she admired and with whom she corresponded, it was said, "Throughout his life a sense of humour, fantastic and peculiarly his own, flickered over and illuminated all he said and did, even when he was desperately in

earnest. Like St. Teresa or Blessed Thomas More
he thought that a man's religion was likely to be all
the more sincere if he was able to make jokes about
it."[1]

Mr. Cowper Powys has suggested that the pro-
foundest definition of *homo sapiens* is the description
of him as the "animal who laughs"; and he gives us
the clue to the humour of the saints by asking, "Is it
not a certain absorbed preoccupation with other
people's attitude to ourselves that most of all puts a
damper upon humour?" Detachment is its secret.
Free from personal egotism, Evelyn Underhill could
see the world in its right proportions and perspective.
In this, according to the bold opinion of Dean
Matthews, she was sharing the divine point of view:
"Clearly a human being is imperfect who lacks a gift
of humour, and without irreverence it may be
supposed that the ground of this good gift is in
God."[2]

II

Obviously, Evelyn Underhill was greater than her
books; but I write as one who only knew her through
her books. There they stand facing me in a row in
order of their publication, thirty-three of them,
exclusive of booklets but inclusive of the two pseudo-
anonymous volumes with the name of John Cordelier
on the title-page. They begin with the collection of
humorous verse, *A Bar-Lamb's Ballad Book* (1902)
and end with her *Letters* (1943), admirably edited and
prefaced by Mr. Charles Williams in 1943, and *Light
of Christ*, published in 1944.

---

[1] *Spiritual Letters of Dom John Chapman*, p. viii.
[2] Matthews, *God in Christian Thought*, p. 244.

Most interesting it is to trace the development of her enlarging mind as she gave utterance to her deepest convictions. At one and the same time she reflects the general sequence of theological thought in her generation and also serves to direct it. During the last thirty years Christian theology has become increasingly "orthodox" and more and more "incarnational." The same process may be paralleled in her thought. Her humility enabled her mind to go on expanding and assimilating to the end. By the time she had begun to write she had outgrown her early agnosticism, and was Neo-Platonic in temper and outlook. This phase continued until the end of the last war. During this period she wrote three novels and two volumes of poetry; her great and epoch-making *Mysticism* (1911); her two Cordelier books, *The Spiral Way* and *The Path of the Eternal Wisdom*, which in later life she came to dislike for reasons which are obvious but not at all convincing, and *The Mystic Way* (1913) in which she accepted a modernist view of the Gospels which Liberal-Protestantism had made popular but which is now definitely out-of-date. In *Practical Mysticism* (1914) and the two Ruysbroeck books (1915 and 1916) she was still only a Christian in a vague sense; but she was now coming increasingly under the influence of Baron von Hügel, and signs of it begin to appear in her study of *Jacopone da Todi* (1919) and *The Essentials of Mysticism* in 1920. By 1922 the Rubicon has been passed: her thought is now patently incarnational and institutional.

F. W. H. Myers characterized the three intellectual virtues as "Curiosity, Candour and Care." Evelyn Underhill had them in an exceptional degree. They explain the progress of her mind. The development in her thought was due to an innate docility and honesty, and to an amazing industry, by which, without any special academic training, she gained her wide and deep and accurate knowledge of theology. (It may be noted here that in 1922 she was the first woman lecturer to have her name on the Oxford University list; and later on, the first woman to become a Fellow of King's College, London, and one of the few to be a Doctor of Divinity of the University of Aberdeen.) Her erudition was almost frightening. Even as early as 1911 in the bibliographical notes at the end of *Mysticism*, one can see the immense range of her reading in several languages; and she steadily added to her stores of learning as the years passed.

A note has been preserved of what might be called her "first conversion" in 1907, when she had "an overpowering vision which really had no specifically Christian elements," though it convinced her that the Catholic religion was true. No definite moment is noted of the later change, but by 1922 the Catholic religion filled the whole horizon of her mind and she had become a devout and practising member of the Church of England. It is deeply significant that in the first book published after this change, in 1922, *The Life of the Spirit and the Life of To-day*, one of the chapters is entitled "Institutional Religion and the Life of the Spirit"; and that the next book was *The Mystics of the Church* (1925). In 1926 came evidence of a new activity in a little volume called *Concerning the Inner Life*, the first-fruits of the Retreats which she was now beginning to conduct with increasing frequency. *Man and the Supernatural*, in 1927, made obvious the immense debt she owed to Baron von Hügel, who had died two years before.

Unfortunately, it met with a lukewarm reception; but it is now recognized as one of the most important of her lesser books, forming an admirable introduction to the philosophy of religion. Several smaller books appeared during the following eight years and then came the second of her two great works, with the significant title *Worship* (1936). When one compares this with *Mysticism*, the chief book of her earlier period, then the immense change of emphasis which has taken place in the intervening years is immediately obvious. The latter book is predominantly incarnational, institutional and sacramental. The words used are different; for example, the word "reality" which occurs so frequently in her first books is almost entirely absent. There is less stress on mysticism. It is strange to notice that the word is not to be found in the index, nor the word "contemplation." To a youthful reader the style of the book may seem flat compared with the earlier: there are no purple passages; but its deeper maturity makes this authoritative statement of her final point of view a much sounder exposition of the fundamental facts of life and religion. When one compares her study of the Gospels in *The Mystic Way* with her discussion of the doctrine of the Incarnation in *Worship*, the contrast shows how immensely she had grown in wisdom and spiritual insight.

In her last years she published four lesser books which give a key to the deepest convictions of her mind and the fundamental basis of her spirit. In four Broadcast Talks given in 1937 under the general title *The Spiritual Life*, she outlines the main structure by which the soul of man is supported in his commerce with Eternity. In *The Mystery of Sacrifice* (1938) and in *Eucharistic Prayers from the Ancient*

Liturgies (1939) she admits us to the inmost sanctities of her sacramental experience. Increasingly her spiritual life centred round the Altar: it seemed an appropriate coincidence that she died within the Octave of Corpus Christi and one turns back to the poem on that Feast in her earlier volume of verse:

. . . . .

Yea, I have understood
    How all things are one great oblation made:
He on our altars, we on the world's rood.
Even as this corn,
Earth-born,
We are snatched from the sod;
Reaped, ground to grist,
Crushed and tormented in the Mills of God,
And offered at Life's hands, a living Eucharist.[1]

In 1940, after the outbreak of war, *Abba* was printed. With a sublime simplicity she brings us back to the prayer of childhood in which as children we were already introduced to the divinest wisdom of the world. About the same time several volumes by other writers appeared dealing with the "Prayer that teaches to pray"; but there are two which have something distinctively new to say—Gerald Heard's *The Creed of Christ* and Evelyn Underhill's *Abba*.

Since her death, *The Fruits of the Spirit* has been published (1942), containing Retreat Addresses as well as the intimate and inimitable letters addressed to the young members of the Prayer Group which was one of the main concerns of her last years of life. The year 1943 saw the publication of her *Letters* and 1944 the *Light of Christ*, a book small in size but transmitting the radiance of Eternity, the *Lumen Christi*.

[1] *Immanence*, p. 81.

It may, then, justifiably be thought that this present collection of articles and this introduction are superfluous. Can anything new be added to what has already been made public? Perhaps not; and yet there are two reasons for this new volume. (1) It contains the very core of her teaching in a form likely to appeal to readers who might be mistrustful of their capacity to grapple with her longer works, and for whom in their diffident humility she has a very special message. And (2) every new book that is published is likely to find a certain number of new readers. It is hoped that in this case the new readers who are introduced for the first time to Evelyn Underhill will find in it only the beginning of an increasingly grateful and gratified exploration of the rich treasure awaiting them in her other books.

This volume brings together a selection of scattered articles on the subject of prayer, worship, and the spiritual life of the teacher, articles which were likely to be forgotten unless revived in this form. In *The Essentials of Mysticism* Evelyn Underhill lamented that "the majority of the 'well-educated' probably pass through life without any knowledge of the science of prayer, with at best the vaguest notions of the hygiene of the soul." In this book will be found several of her efforts to teach this science to amateurs and to recommend this hygiene. What she says will come home with most force to those who know something of her general point of view; and therefore it has been thought worth while to preface these articles with a short outline of the main features of her teaching.

B

III

It may be that some will question the wisdom of publishing such a book as this at such a time as this when men's minds are stunned almost into insensibility by the calamities which have crashed upon the world,[1] and when even the desire to pray seems thwarted by the lack of leisure to pursue it. As Evelyn Underhill said of one of her books published during the last war:

> "Many will feel that in such a time of conflict and horror when only the most ignorant, disloyal or apathetic can hope for quietness of mind, a book which deals with that which is called the 'contemplative' attitude to existence is wholly out of place."

But, as our study of her teaching soon makes plain, the one hope for the future depends on the contemplative attitude to life. If this world is to be saved it can only be by the intrusion of another world into it—a world of higher truth and greater reality than that which is now submerged by the overwhelming disharmonies and sufferings of the present time. Teaching about prayer, far from being irrelevant, is the teaching most needed at the moment. It should never be forgotten that it has been at periods which seem most destructive and disastrous that the mystical consciousness has been at its most sensitive awareness. For example, in the third century, when the despotism of the emperors gave small scope for an active career, Plotinus explored an other-dimensional universe and brought

[1] This was written in 1944.

back authentic news of its conditions. During the desolation of the Great Interdict in the fourteenth century, Tauler, Ruysbroeck and Suso were pioneers in the internal ways of the Spirit and opened them up for others. Amid the horrors of the English civil wars Walter Hilton and the Lady Julian had their transcendental experiences and made them available for others. All this may encourage us who are overwhelmed by the contemporary catastrophe, to seek and to find the deep wells of vitality which will make us more steadfast and efficient members of the human family. Evelyn Underhill will uncover them for us. Putting ourselves with an eager and supple docility at her side she will enaole us to have at least a glimpse of her vision and a first-hand perception of the "World-unwalled" in which she habitually lived. Her guidance will teach her pupils "to see this world in a truer proportion, discerning eternal beauty beyond and beneath apparent ruthlessness. It will educate them in a charity free from taint of sentimentalism; it will confer on them an unconquerable hope; and assure them that still, even in this hour of greatest desolation, 'there lives the dearest freshness deep down things.'"[1]

The subjects on which she wrote may be broadly divided under two heads, God and the Soul.

GOD

Her thought in every phase of its development is pre-eminently theocentric. Adoration is the prevailing attitude of mind. It is the central word, reiterated again and again, of her great book on *Worship*. A comment on Alice Meynell in the *New Statesman* is exactly applicable to Evelyn Underhill: "She has a

[1] *Practical Mysticism*, p. xi.

curious intimacy with tremendous things, a touch at once adoring and familiar." Awe, contrition, diffidence are joined with eagerness, thrill and confidence. In describing Ruysbroeck she unwittingly describes herself: "Awe and rapture, theological profundity, keen psychological insight are tempered by a touching simplicity. We listen to the report of one who has indeed heard 'the invitation of love' which draws interior souls towards the One and says 'Come home.' A humble receptivity, a meek self-naughting is with Ruysbroeck, as with all great mystics, the gate of the City of God. Because they have given themselves to God in every action, omission or submission . . . they possess a peace and a joy, a consolation and a savour, that none can comprehend; neither the world, nor the creature adorned for himself nor whosoever prefers himself before God."[1] These qualities of her heart qualify everything she writes, testifying to her direct knowledge of the truth which she proclaims.

What she emphasizes is the reality, the supremacy and the accessibility of God.

(1) The word "reality" is found frequently in her earlier books; it is significant that she came to use it less and less. But as used by her it is free from the pantheistic error which a less discriminating mind might easily associate with it. Even in her more distinctly Neo-Platonic days she was in no danger of depersonalizing the Deity or blurring the distinction between Him and His creatures. In contradiction to what Reinhold Niebuhr says about Mysticism, by her "the finite world" was never "regarded as illusory or evil"; nor was "the eternal world regarded as a

[1] *Mysticism*, p. 505.

realm of undifferentiated unity from which the particularity, individuality and insufficiency of the finite world have been expunged."[1] By the word "reality" she wished to connote the eternal Self-subsistence and Self-sufficiency of God; it emphasized His transcendence without excluding His immanence.

Coventry Patmore defined mysticism as "the science of reality"; Evelyn Underhill spoke of it as "the art of union with reality"; to both of them the ultimate reality is God. In *Mysticism* she quotes from *The Rod, the Root and the Flower*—"God is the only Reality; and we are real only so far as we are in His order and He is in us."[2]

(2) From this it follows that God is not only (to use von Hügel's phrase) "a stupendously rich Reality," but the supreme Lord of creation and the ultimate good of the human race. While not sympathizing with Barth's irrationalism she could sympathize (within limits) with his insistence on God as "the Wholly Other." She had two things on which Niebuhr lays stress as conditions of a true religion: "The first is the sense of reverence for a majesty and of dependence upon an ultimate source of being. The second is the sense of moral obligation laid upon one from beyond oneself and of moral unworthiness before a judge."[3]

In her earlier period Evelyn Underhill collaborated with Rabindranath Tagore in editing the Poems of Kabir, the fifteenth-century Hindu ascetic; in her later stage she edited prayers from the Eastern Liturgies, which acclaim the Incarnate Christ as Lord of all the world, the supreme Good. In both phases of her thought her mind and heart are set

[1] Niebuhr, *The Christian View of Man*, vol. i, p. 145.
[2] *The Rod, the Root and the Flower*, p. 172. [3] Niebuhr, op. cit., p. 141.

towards God as the final Arbiter, the absolute Prize and the Alpha and Omega of the soul's quest—the supreme "Joy of man's desiring"; and in an ecstasy of joy in discovering what He is she breaks out:

> Not to me
> The Unmoved Mover of philosophy
> And absolute still sum of all that is,
> The God whom I adore—not this.
> Nay, rather a great moving wave of bliss,
> A surging torrent of dynamic love
> In passionate swift career,
> That down the sheer
> And fathomless abyss
> Of Being ever pours, his ecstasy to prove.[1]

(3) She emphasizes the accessibility of God in that she expresses and expounds the Biblical view of the "Living God"; and as the Living God, "in Him we live and move and have our being." Infinitely pervasive, He is intimately accessible, not waiting passively to be sought but actively stimulating and alluring the soul. The thought of His initiative and prevenience is inextricably bound up with her view of His reality and supremacy and inwardness. Her emphasis on it deepened. In a new edition of *Mysticism* published in 1930 she said that if she were replanning the book more stress would be laid on "the predominant part played in the soul's development by the free and prevenient action of the Supernatural as against all merely evolutionary or emergent theories of spiritual transcendence."

In one of her Broadcast Talks she has this significant passage: "In all the records of those who have

[1] *Theophanies*, p. 3.

had this experience (i.e. of conversion) we notice that there is always the sense that we are concerned with two realities, not one: that while it is true that there is something in man which longs for the Perfect and can move towards it, what matters most and takes precedence of all else is the fact of a living Reality over against man, who stoops towards him and first incites and then supports and responds to his seeking."[1]

And in *Abba* she has a whole chapter on the subject under the head of "Prevenience."

She illuminates with a fresh beauty the truth of His Immanence, which she takes as the title of her first book of Poems. Some of her loveliest and best known are on this theme, such as "The Uxbridge Road," or "I come in the little things," or "What do you seek within, O Soul, my brother?" Here is another, written in 1924:

VENI CREATOR
(For Whitsun Eve)

Come with birds' voices when the light grows dim
  Yet lovelier in departure and more dear:
While the warm flush hangs yet at heaven's rim
  And the one star shines clear.

Tho' the swift night haste to approaching day
  Stay Thou and stir not, brooding on the deep;
In secret love, Thy silent word let say
  Within the senses' sleep

Softer than dew. But when the morning wind
  Blows down the world, O Spirit, show Thy power:
Quicken the dreams within the languid mind
  And bring Thy seed to flower.

[1] *The Spiritual Life*, p. 56.

Any danger of an excessive individualism or unhealthy introspection in this thought of the divine inwardness was overcome in her acceptance of the Church's teaching of the sacraments and the corporate fellowship. And similarly any danger of an excessive emotionalism or reliance on "spiritual feelings" was also removed in the later stage of her teaching. In *Practical Mysticism* she had opened the door to misunderstanding by quoting with approval John Keats's aspiration: "O for a life of sensation rather than of thought." Unless carefully interpreted and discriminatingly understood, this might easily lead the novice to strain after abnormal experiences, bereft of which he would feel himself abandoned. Evelyn Underhill counterbalanced this ambiguity by presenting the other point of view in *Worship*. She quotes the statement of St. Francis de Sales that "he had no sensible devotion in prayer," combining this with some words of Père Grou (who in her later life seems to have taken the place of the earlier mystics in her regard) to suggest "how little the Christian life of personal devotion is concerned with conscious spiritual contacts or achievements; how entirely its emphasis lies on loving subordination to God, a quiet acceptance of 'the sacrament of the present moment' as a major means of grace, whatever its form. Here the personal response of the individual life follows the great rhythm of the Church's liturgical life."

THE SOUL

The sub-title of her first great book, *Mysticism, A Study of the Nature and Development of Man's Spiritual Consciousness*, covers the topic which, closely connected with the first, was the second dominant interest of her life. She sought to lead her readers to that dimension of being to which we really belong but of which we only gradually become aware—"the Eternal World of ultimate values. The life which we lead as sentient beings in the midst of material things is but the outer edge of a reality which gives to them their meaning."

All her striving was towards the "development of man's spiritual consciousness"; for it was to his failure to develop this that she traced all the tragedies which have overtaken civilization. "There is," she says, "a common idea that the spiritual life means something pious and mawkish: not very desirable in girls and most objectionable in boys."[1] In consequence, the purpose of the universe has been thwarted and the process of evolution checked. If by "Reality" we mean God and His Creation, we can see in the upward push of the universe His training of man for the life of the spirit—our growth into a higher order of reality. According to Evelyn Underhill, the spiritual life is not primarily a matter of history but of biology.[2] We shall not be able to make sense of the tangle of material which is before us until we see in it one ruling principle, one Transcendent Power working and striving towards one end. Not only is there our "normal" consciousness dealing with the external world, but there is also another consciousness (which ought by now to have become equally "normal") dealing with a higher plane of values: "Normal consciousness sorts out some elements from the mass of experiences beating at our doors and constructs from them a certain order; but this order lacks any deep meaning or true cohesion, because normal consciousness is incapable of apprehending

[1] *Essentials of Mysticism*, p. 90.   [2] *Life of the Spirit*, p. 1.

the underlying reality from which these scattered experiences proceed. The claim of the mystical consciousness is to a closer reading of truth; to an apprehension of the divine unifying principle behind appearance. . . . To know this at first hand—not to guess, believe or accept, but to be certain—is the highest achievement of human consciousness and the ultimate object of mysticism."[1]

In this the "push" comes from God. Once again we must insist on the divine initiative, and beware of Pelagianism. When men respond to this higher awareness and desire it, the road is the same for each. There are none who are entirely incapable of it. "The spring of the amazing energy which enables the great mystic to rise to freedom and dominate his world, is latent in all of us, an integral part of our humanity."[2] "Therefore it is to a practical mysticism that the practical man is here invited: to a training of his latent faculties, a bracing and brightening of his languid consciousness, an emancipation from the fetters of appearance, a turning of the attention to new levels of the world. Thus he may become aware of the universe which the spiritual artist is always trying to disclose to the race. This amount of mystical perception—this 'ordinary contemplation' as the specialists call it—is possible to all men; without it they are not wholly conscious, nor wholly alive."[3] "Awakening, Discipline, Enlightenment, Self-surrender and Union are the essential processes of life's response to this fundamental fact."[4]

These activities are generally formulated under three classical heads: Purgation, Illumination and Union, the way of the Beginner, the Learner and the

---

[1] *Essentials*, p. 7. [2] *Mysticism*, p. 532.
[3] *Practical Mysticism*, p. 11. [4] *Mysticism*, p. 534.

Proficient. In all her books up to the cardinal year 1922, she makes much of this threefold scheme. "We must agree that a formula of this kind is not likely to survive for nearly two thousand years unless it agrees with the facts. Those who use it with the greatest conviction are not theorists. They are the practical mystics who are intent in making maps of the regions into which they have penetrated."[1] In her later works Evelyn Underhill laid less stress on the distinctions between these three definite stages. It is as if she became aware that truth cannot be summed up in a formula nor life reduced to a system. But the general sequence of the soul's progress she kept to the end. In *The Golden Sequence* she treats of the soul's progress under two heads only, Purification and Prayer. This simplification does not imply that her aspiration Godwards was less soaring, or her mind more pedestrian; but that now she spoke with a greater simplicity because of a more extended knowledge of the Infinite Abyss of the Godhead and the finite creatureliness of the human soul. In her Introduction to the English translation of Malaval's *Method of Raising the Soul to Contemplation*, she shows that she, as he, "is keenly alive to the diversity between spirits, and anxious to safeguard the rightful liberty of each" (p. xiii). She uses the word "supple" more than once to denote a healthy feature of the spiritual life. Therefore no "system," however accredited by long years of hallowed use, must be imposed arbitrarily.

In the direction to individual souls of which her *Letters* are full there is never anything forced or artificial. Once again, in her Introduction to Malaval she speaks of "that tranquil death to self" which he

[1] *Essentials of Mysticism*, p. 8.

set so high in the ranks of the spiritual virtues; and here the word to be emphasized is "tranquil."

But before leaving this aspect of her teaching it is worth while noting that when she did take a time-honoured formula for the spiritual life she respected it by taking it seriously and trying to translate its terms into practical language for daily use. Thus, in several of her books she makes a good deal of the three "Evangelical Counsels," Poverty, Chastity and Obedience, showing that on a spiritual interpretation they apply to Christians in the world no less than to those in the cloister. "By Poverty the mystic means an utter self-stripping, the casting-off of immaterial as well as material wealth, a complete detachment from all finite things. By Chastity he means an extreme and limpid purity of soul, virgin to all but God; by Obedience, that abnegation of selfhood that mortification of the will which results in a complete humility, a 'holy indifference' to the accidents of life." So she wrote in *Mysticism* (p. 247). She says in *The Essentials of Mysticism* (p. 13): "The monastic rule of poverty, chastity and obedience aims at the removal of those self-centred desires and attachments which chain consciousness to a personal instead of a universal life. He who no longer craves for personal possessions, pleasures or powers, is very near to perfect liberty." In *Jacopone da Todi* she reiterates the same truth in different words (p. 91): "That threefold vow of poverty, chastity and obedience, which summarises the demands of Christian asceticism, represents not merely three external obligations, but three essential interior conditions of the soul which seeks for union with God. They are interdependent forms of spiritual freedom, based on the liberating virtue of humility." And at the very end of her life, in her last letter but one to the members of her "Prayer Group," written in Lent, 1941, she devoted nearly the whole of the letter to a fresh paraphrase of the imperative demands made by the three "Counsels" to every serious-minded follower of our Lord.

From even this slight sketch of Evelyn Underhill's teaching, it is clear that to her belonged in an eminent degree that "temper of soul" with which she credited the great French directors of the spiritual life. Nothing could more adequately sum up her own essential characteristics—that which constitutes her secret—than what she says of this temper in her Introduction to the English translation of Abbé de Tourville's *Letters of Direction*:

"It is marked by a twofold realism. On the one hand by a vivid sense of the presence and transcendence of God, a confident self-giving to God, as the essence of religion. On the other hand by an acceptance of human nature as it really is, in its limitations and weakness, and a determination to find the raw material of its sanctification in the homely circumstances of everyday life; yet without any reduction of the splendour of its supernatural destiny. The emphasis in fact lies on the Reality of God, His intimate and over-ruling action; and on that humble acceptance of the facts of our situation which the Baron von Hügel called 'a creaturely sense.' With this balanced and deeply Christian outlook goes a method of direction which is perhaps specially appropriate to our own times; a robust common-sense, a touch which is firm yet delicate, a wise tolerance of human weakness, a perpetual recourse

to facts, a hatred of moral and devotional pettiness."

In saying that, she might have been writing her own
obituary notice. That is how we think of her, those
who had the opulent privilege of being her personal
friends and those who never knew her but bear the
grave responsibility of having been inspired by her
and owing her what can never be reckoned.

Εὐχαριστῶ τῷ θεῷ μου ἐπὶ πάσῃ τῇ μνείᾳ ὑνῶν.[1]

In conclusion we repeat the prayer which was
offered in the Chapel she loved and sanctified at
Pleshey when her memorial was dedicated there:

O God, who by the lives of those who love Thee dost
    refashion the souls of men,
We give Thee thanks for the ministry of Thy servant
    Evelyn;
In whose life and words Thy love and majesty were
    made known to us,
Whose loving spirit set our spirits on fire,
Who learnt from Thee the Shepherd's care for His
    sheep;
Grant that some measure of the Spirit which she
    received from Thee may fall on us who loved
    her.
We ask it for the sake of Jesus Christ our Lord.
                             Amen.

                  LUMSDEN, ST. ANDREWS

---

[1] Philippians i. 3.

LIFE AS PRAYER
AND OTHER WRITINGS OF
EVELYN UNDERHILL

EDITOR'S NOTE

THE papers collected in this volume were written by Evelyn Underhill during the years 1922 to 1937. The reason why she did not include the earlier ones in her collection of Essays and Addresses, published in 1933 under the title *Mixed Pasture*, was that most of them, first given as Lectures or Addresses, were published as pamphlets and were then having an active career of their own.

Four of the papers are concerned chiefly with prayer; one (*The Inside of Life*) with the lives of "dwellers in time who are yet capable of Eternity"; one (*Worship*) is addressed to students of religion who are trying to *live* religion: one (*What is Mysticism?*) deals with what Baron von Hügel called "the metaphysical thirst": while the last three treat of the vocation and spiritual outlook of the teacher.

I

THE DEGREES OF PRAYER[1]

THE subject of this paper is man's fundamental spiritual activity—*prayer*. Every religious mind is, of course, familiar with the idea of prayer; and in one degree or another, with the practice of it. Yet we sometimes forget how very little we really know about it; how personal and subjective are the accounts spiritual writers give of it; how empirical and how obscure in its deepest moments, even for the best of us, our own understanding of it must be. Here we are, little half-animal, half-spiritual creatures, mysteriously urged from within and enticed from without to communion with spiritual reality. If and when we surrender to this craving and this attraction, we enter thereby—though at first but dimly—on a completely new life, full of variety, of new joy, tension and pain, and offering an infinite opportunity of development to us. Such is the life of prayer, as understood by the mystics, and as practised with greater or less completeness of surrender and reward by all real lovers of Christ.

Now because of its truly living richness and variety, these men and women of prayer do not always describe their experience in the same way. Hence the attempt which is made in many devotional books to reduce their statements to a system, turn their art into a science, often leads to failure and confusion. I do not want, primarily, to study and compare these specialists, or discuss the subject of prayer in too

[1] Printed for the Guild of Health, 1922.

technical a way; though we cannot avoid some use of psychology if we are to bring it into line with our thoughts about other aspects of life—a mental necessity for us all. I wish rather to consider our own prayerful activities in the light of the certain fact that there *are* quite definite and different grades and sorts of prayer, which do appear to be the normal expressions of different grades and sorts of souls at various periods of their growth. It seems to me well that all those truly in earnest about the practice of the inner life, and especially those trying to help other souls, should realize and study this; not in order that we may always be feeling our own devotional pulses —for nothing is worse than that—but in order that we may learn to deal wisely with our own souls, and better understand the problems of those who come to us for help. Surely all Christians ought to possess a general conception of the normal development of the religious consciousness; and this conception should be present with us, as a general conception of the right functioning of the body is present with us. It should govern our own prayer, truing up and correcting it, and control all our dealings with the problems of the spiritual life.

In prayer, we open up our souls to the Divine energy and grace perpetually beating in on us; and receive that energy and grace, in order that it may be transmuted by our living zest into work—may cleanse, invigorate and slowly change us. It is therefore of primary importance to all Christians to know how best to set up and maintain the contacts of prayer. This is a difficult art—we should bring intelligence as well as love to bear on it. It is all very well to say that you will find it all in St. Teresa. For persons of mature experience, the writings of

St. Teresa are the most exact of guides; but they are guides to the mountains, and can be misunderstood by the novice, or even lead into danger those who are hasty and untrained. Emotional temperaments, too, can find in such books an excuse for revelling in mere devotionalism; and this is contrary to the true ethos of Christian spirituality. Christian spirituality seeks union with God in order that we may better serve the purposes of His will; and one of the ways in which this is done is by the expansion of the prayerful consciousness. Anything, therefore, which we can find out about this is a true extension of our knowledge of the Kingdom of Heaven.

The first thing that occurs to us is, that all the machinery of prayer has but one very simple object— our loving intercourse with God—and that all progress in it can be described as an increased closeness in the intercourse and an increased perfection in the love. The varieties and degrees of the machinery have in themselves no intrinsic importance, except in so far as they contribute to this. We study them, as we study the normal development of bodily or mental activity, because we find, in practice, that they occur; and it is better and more healthy to know this, than to be baffled and puzzled when, for instance, we find ourselves for the first time plunged in the prayer of simplicity, and unable to make use of our ordinary forms. But, in considering our own prayer, it is of little importance to ask ourselves whether we have attained this or that degree, but of great importance to ask ourselves what is the condition and attitude of our souls in the degree which we find ourselves to be practising—whether this prayer is truly humbling, bracing, and vivifying us, or merely inducing a state of emotional languor or spiritual strain. All the greatest masters of prayer bring home to us the simple, natural, unforced character of real intercourse with God. They say again and again that prayer is nothing else but a devout intent directed towards Him; and this intent expresses itself in various ways. The beginner must be shown these ways, and often be helped to use them; but in the mature man or woman of prayer their exercise is free and spontaneous. Perhaps there is no other department of the spiritual life in which St. Augustine's great saying, "Love, and do what you like," becomes more completely true. Julian of Norwich says at the end of her Revelations, that what she has found and felt most fully is "the homeliness, courtesy and naturehood of God." So the soul's real progress is not towards some mysterious, abnormal and trance-like condition; but rather towards the unspoilt, trustful, unsophisticated apprehension of the little child. This is what matters; not the special degree in which it is experienced. Thus a badly held, distracted attempt at the prayer of simplicity, involving tension and effort, and therefore self-consciousness, has far less spiritual content than an unforced, humble and natural vocal prayer. In prayer, will and grace co-operate. Neither a limp abandonment to the supposed direction of the Spirit, nor a vigorous determinatoin to wrestle with God on our own account, will do for it. Our willed self-donation conditions the reception of grace: grace conditions the power of the prayerful will. Hence it is useless to endeavour by willed struggle, or by obeying the rules in ascetic manuals, to reach a level of prayer to which we are not yet impelled by grace. We cannot by stretching ourselves add an inch to our stature: the result will be strain, not growth. All this means that we should be very chary of taking at face value the advice given in little books about "going into the silence" and so on: and should never treat this advice as though it were applicable to every soul at every time. Real inward silence is not achieved by any deliberate spiritual trick. It develops naturally; and most often from the full exercise of mental prayer, which is in its turn the child of properly practised vocal prayer. Therefore I think that no one ought to set to work to practise such inward silence until they feel a strong impulse so to do. If we try such artificial methods, we probably drift into a mere quietistic reverie; and such reverie, though pleasant, has nothing in common with real contemplative prayer.

So, we shall do best if we enter on the study of the degrees of prayer safeguarded by this principle: that whilst keeping in mind the highest ideal of attainment, we are never to struggle for a degree or condition of fervour in which we do not naturally find ourselves. People are often encouraged to do this by indiscriminate reading of ascetic and mystical literature, a practice to which real dangers are attached. They browse among descriptions and counsels intended only for advanced souls, and struggle to produce states of consciousness far beyond their power. These states will arise within us naturally and simply, only when and if we are ready for them. In all normal cases, God feeds and leads the soul very gently. Growth is gradual. The many adjustments necessary to the full establishment of the prayerful consciousness take time; and often its advance is checked by periods of dullness, fatigue and incapacity which are explicable by psychology, and must be borne with patience as instruments of our purification. All the great masters of prayer refer to them, and insist, too, that humble surrender, not constant fervour, is the best index of the soul's good-will. Thus Walter Hilton says: "When thou disposest thee to think of God, if thy heart be dull and dark, and feels neither wit nor savour nor devotion for to think, but only a bare desire and a weak will that thou wouldst think of God, but thou canst not—then I hope it is good to thee that thou strive not much with thyself, as if thou wouldst by thine own might overcome thyself." Here Hilton shows himself to be intuitively aware of that which psychologists now call the law of Reversed Effort— the fact that such desperate striving with ourselves merely frustrates its own end, and increases our baffled sense of helplessness. And again, to the soul dissatisfied with its ordinary prayers and hankering after contemplation, he says: "Press not too much thereafter, as if thou wert abiding or gaping after some strange stirring or some wonderful feeling other than thou hast had." And another old English mystic tells us not to be like "greedy greyhounds" snatching at God's gifts, but to come gently and willingly to His outstretched hand and take what He gives us.

Psychology could gloss all these counsels, and prove their validity from its own point of view. Indeed, the more we read of the directions for education and practice in prayer which are given by the mystics, the more we are struck by their psychological exactitude. All that we are at present able to say about the technique of prayer and contemplation as a part of the psychology of religious experience has been said by them more beautifully and incisively. I think that nothing gives one more strongly the sense of belonging to a supernatural society committed to the practice of the spiritual life than the discovery of this identity: finding on one hand our own difficulties and errors noted and dealt with centuries ago, on the other hand those psychological conceptions of the unconscious, of affective thought and of suggestion, which we like to think so modern, merely translating the discoveries of the mystics into the language of the present day. The degrees of prayer can therefore be described either in terms of psychology or in terms of grace. We ought, I think, to study them on both levels; for the more we are able to come to terms with modern forms of expression the more we are likely to be able to spread the news of the Kingdom of God.

We take, then, as our first principle the humble and diligent use of the degree of prayer natural to a soul at any particular stage of its course, and not the anxious straining towards some other degree yet beyond it: and as our second principle, that prayer has its psychological as well as its spiritual side, and in the effort to understand it better we should keep our eye on both. It has been well said that our Lord in all His acts and teaching kept His eye on *man* as he really is; and here, in particular, we should make a humble but persistent effort to follow Him. From this point we can go on to consider what the degrees of prayer really are. Spiritual writers give them various names and divisions, but as a matter of fact they shade into one another, forming, as it were, a sliding scale from the simplest prayer of the Christian child to the infused contemplation of the soul absorbed in God. I propose now to make five divisions: and these are—Vocal Prayer, Meditation, the Prayer of Immediate Acts, the Prayer of Simplicity, the Prayer of Quiet. Beyond these are the higher degrees of contemplation, which are outside our present scope.

First, then, comes Vocal Prayer. We all know what this is; but we do not always remember, in our eagerness for something more spiritual, that apart from its devotional aspect its educative value for the soul that uses it is greater than is sometimes supposed. In vocal prayer we speak, not only to God, but also to ourselves. We are filling our minds with acts of love, praise, humility and penitence, which will serve us well in times when the power of mental prayer seems to fail us and the use of these formulas becomes the only way of turning to God left within our reach. Moreover, psychology insists that the spoken word has more suggestive power, is more likely to reach and modify our deeper psychic levels, than any inarticulate thought; for the centres of speech are closely connected with the heart of our mental life. Therefore those who value the articulate recitation of a daily office, the use of litanies and psalms, are keeping closer to the facts of existence than those who only talk generally of remaining in a state of prayer. I feel sure that some vocal prayer should enter into the daily rule even of the most contemplative soul. It gives shape and discipline to our devotions, and keeps us in touch with the great traditions of the Church. Moreover, such vocal prayers, if we choose them well, have the evocative quality of poetry: they rouse the dormant spiritual sense, and bring us into the presence of God. "Oft it falls," says Hilton, "that praying with thy mouth gets and keeps fervour of devotion, and if a man cease from saying, devotion vanishes away."

As the life of prayer begins to exert its full power, such vocal prayers will gradually but steadily become slower and more pondered. The soul finds in their phrases more and more significance, makes of these phrases special applications, and is led on by them to petitions and aspirations of its own. This means that it is drawing near to the next stage, that of meditation. This is the first degree of mental prayer; that is to say, prayer in which we do not repeat set forms, but do something on our own account. Meditation is a word which covers a considerable range of devotional states. It is perhaps most simply defined as thinking in the Presence of God. And since our ordinary thoughts are scattered, seldom poised for long on one point, but evoked and influenced by a multitude of external things, real meditation requires as its preliminary what ascetic writers call recollection—a deliberate gathering of ourselves together, a retreat into our own souls. This is more easily done by a simple exercise of the imagination, a gentle turning to God, than by those ferocious efforts towards concentrating which some manuals advise, and which often end by concentrating attention on the concentration itself. I will not go further into their technical descriptions of method; which seem so difficult when we read them, and often worry people needlessly. There is no virtue in any one method, except in so far as it succeeds; and different methods succeed with different souls. For some, the slow reading of a passage in the Bible or the *Imitation* leads directly to a state of prayer: for others, a quiet dwelling on one of God's attributes is a gateway to adoration. Articulate speech is now left aside, but the ceaseless stream of inward discourse may persist, and become a secret conversation with God; while others will be led to consideration, a quiet ruminating on spiritual things. As to Three-point Meditations and so on, it is perhaps enough if we keep in mind that every real meditation, however short, natural and artless, does involve three points: for our mind, will and feelings are all exercised in it. We think in some way of the subject of our meditation. We feel the emotion, whether of love, penitence or joy, which it suggests to us. And finally, the aim of all meditative prayer is a resolution, or a renewal of our surrender to God: and this is an act of the will.

Practically every person who prays at all, and has not reached one of the stages of contemplative prayer, can meditate in a simple way if he chooses to practise this art; and it is most fruitful, especially perhaps in the early stages of the spiritual life, whilst the purgation and remaking of character is still in the foreground. It comes naturally to people of active minds, the reasoners, and the ponderers; who have only to occupy their normal thinking powers on spiritual material for a set period of each day in order to develop it. Many souls remain in this type of prayer throughout their spiritual course. Within its own limitations it gives ample scope for variety; and this is a great need if the life of prayer is to be kept in a wholesome state. It can be applied to a wide range of subjects and conditions of the soul; extending from the simplest reflections, considerations and talkings to God, arising often out of our reading or our vocal or liturgic prayer, to the beginnings of those spontaneous acts of the will and heart which are really the first movements towards the next degree of prayer; that is to say, the Prayer of Immediate Acts.

The transition from meditation to immediate acts takes place only in those souls which have some tendency to contemplation; not perhaps much, but still an aptitude seeking expression. By them it is commonly felt as a decreasing inclination to reason or discourse in prayer, and an increasing inclination to simple, spontaneous expressions of love and penitence. It is true that the praying self does think; but not with the same method and completeness as before. It now dwells more and more on the affections; on acts of love and adoration, meek aspirations to God, expressed in short phrases which may seem banal enough when we read them in books of devotion, but become charged, for the soul in this degree, with the most intense significance. We remember the favourite aspiration of St. Francis: "My God, my God, what art Thou and what am I?" Such aspirations, formed from memories of past reading and prayers, rise spontaneously into consciousness as the prayer proceeds; and those whose minds are richly stored with Scripture phrases and liturgic forms will seldom be at a loss for them. They are, however, only the expression of the act. "Press thou towards God with the sharp dart of thy longing love," says the author of *The Cloud of Unknowing* in his directions for this prayer, "and take no thought for words." Intuition here begins to take the place of logical considerations; and, as psychologists would say, affective thought as well as rational thought is taken up into the life of prayer, which now overflows its first boundaries and invades wider and wider regions of the self. As this degree matures in those to whom it is appropriate, the "immediate acts" of the heart decrease and will grow simpler and rarer. There is often a marked distaste and inability for meditation. There are pauses, periods of deep silence, hushed communion which the soul feels to be more and more fruitful. Here we are at the threshold of that progressive absorption which leads to the true contemplative state. Gradually one act of will, affection or aspiration comes more and more to dominate the whole prayer, say of half an hour's duration or more: and is used merely to true up that state of attention which is the very heart of prayer. When this condition is established, the soul has reached the degree which is sometimes called the prayer of simplicity, and sometimes that of repose, simple attention or active contemplation. It is thrown open with great love and desire to God, but in so simple a way that it cannot analyse its own experience. Its whole impulse is to wait on Him rather than to speak to Him. It was in the effort to describe the apprehensions of this degree that the author of *The Cloud of Unknowing* said, "God may well be loved, but not thought. Therefore I will leave all I can think and take to my love that which I cannot think." Nevertheless I am sure it is a mistake to imagine that such prayer can be well developed and preserved, unless a certain care be given to its mental preparation. It is far better to enter it with *some* idea or disposition in the mind, some special thought of God, some distinct orientation of the will, than in the state of vague blankness characteristic of quietism; for this will merely encourage distraction and religious day-dreams, and may even bring about a sort of self-hypnotization. The ultimate object of all prayer is greater efficiency for God, not the limp self-abandonment of quietism; and therefore as the soul approaches the passive degrees a careful discrimination becomes necessary. The direction of the mystics is that we should enter on simple contemplation with "a devout intent directed to God," and there is something very definite about that.

We often confuse ourselves by speaking and thinking of contemplation as a "state." It is not a state
in the sense of being static, a continuous unchanging
condition. In all those degrees of prayer which we
are considering, a constant variety of acts is normal,
wholesome and inevitable. Though a rapt attention
to God dominate the prayer, within this attention
must fluctuate, thoughts and acts must arise from
time to time. To say this is only to say that our
mental life persists in it. Now when these thoughts
and acts, these ripples on the deep pool of contemplation, are born of that profound feeling of charity and
compassion which cannot long remain untouched by
our neighbours' needs and griefs, then surely intercession of the very best kind is exercised by us. For
intercession is a special and deliberate way of
exercising love, in completest union with the Love of
God. And to be in perfect charity with all men is
already to intercede for them; to put, as it were, our
spiritual weight on their side of the scale.

These four degrees of prayer—that is, ordinary
vocal prayer, mental prayer or meditation, immediate
acts, and simplicity—are to a great extent within the
self's control. In theological language they are
natural and not supernatural degrees. Once they are
thoroughly established, the soul can normally and
under suitable conditions produce them. But with
the real Prayer of Quiet, we pass beyond this condition. It is wholly involuntary. None can produce
it of themselves; and it seems always to come as a
distinct and irresistible experience from without. In
technical terms, it is "infused" or the work of grace.
In this real quiet, which may come suddenly upon
the soul in the course of its ordinary prayer, it is
not merely drawn towards a simple and imageless

attention to God and aspiration towards Him. It is more or less intensely aware of His Presence. Here, in fact, we have the first faint emergence of the mystical consciousness, in stillness and humility receiving the obscure impression of the Divine. In the prayer of simplicity and aspiration, the deeps of the unconscious are opened up to God; and that this is veritably done in these degrees is proved by their effect on the impulsive sources of conduct. But in the quiet, and the simple union which is the full development of quiet, this apprehension overflows into consciousness; and this is something which the self cannot effect by the exercise of will. All great writers on prayer insist on this point.

Sometimes the establishment of this new degree comes by way of a painful inward struggle and aridity; what St. John of the Cross has described as "the night of the senses"—a period of distress and obscurity, in which it seems to the soul that it is losing all it had gained of the life of prayer. This is more especially felt by people who have real contemplative aptitude, and whom this type of spirituality is destined in the end to dominate. It meets and must conquer many resistances in their active minds, must cut for itself new paths; and this may involve tension and suffering and the apparent withdrawal of the ordinary power of prayer. Here is a point at which skilled and sympathetic guidance is of special service to the soul, which is often bewildered and disheartened by its own experience, its strange sense of dimness and incapacity. Others, whose natural level is, and may always remain, the prayer of aspiration or of simplicity, may find themselves plunged in the quiet from time to time; and will obtain from this experience a refreshment, power and absolute certitude which the other degrees of prayer cannot give.

Beyond this point it is hardly I think for us, as ordinary Christians, to explore; and indeed, the cold analysis of these living experiences can only be justified by a longing to help other souls on the path which leads to closer knowledge of God. There is real truth in Hilton's warning that "a ransacker of the might of God and His Majesty, without great purity and meekness, shall be overlaid and oppressed of himself." And perhaps nothing could be worse for our own devotional life than perpetual exploration of that which lies far beyond us. But, looking back at the degrees which we have considered, there are two points regarding them which it is well that we should bear in mind. The first is of practical, the second of psychological interest.

The practical point is this. The use of the higher degrees of prayer does not and should not ever mean the total abandonment of the lower degrees. The soul adds on new ways of intercourse; but this does not involve the abolishing of the old ways—that because she has reached the quiet joy of simplicity she is never to use formal prayer, never to discourse or think out her ideas before God, or make deliberate acts of penitence and love. To suppose this is the fundamental error of quietism. The healthiness of our spiritual life, like that of our mental life, depends to a great extent on its suppleness, and on the variety which we are able to impart to it. We should never, therefore, be afraid of such variety, or suppose we are losing ground if we find ourselves again using discursive prayer or formal acts after practising the higher degrees. The mystics are insistent on this point. Thus St. John of the Cross says, that when

D

the soul is not in the prayer of simplicity it "*ought* to avail itself in all its exercises of the help of good thoughts and meditations, according to what brings it the greatest spiritual profit." And St. Teresa still more strongly—"Since God has given the powers of the soul in order that we may use them, and the work of each has its reward, instead of trying to imprison them by a sort of enchantment let them freely perform their ordinary office, until it pleases God to raise them to a higher state."

It is therefore best to be ready to go up and down the ladder of love: sometimes speaking and sometimes listening, sometimes thinking and sometimes resting in the communion which is beyond thought and speech. A quiet and meek retreat to a lower degree of prayer, which one *can* do, is worth far more than the anxious struggle to tune oneself up to a degree which (anyhow for the moment) one cannot do. Self-will in prayer is a subtle temptation, known to most religious people. But there is always some way of turning to God which is within our reach, however distracted or weary we may be: and as a general rule, it is surely better to begin there, quite simply, though the crudity and childishness of our level of feeling and expression may deal a smart blow at our self-respect. Constituted as we are, it is inevitable that our spiritual aptitude should fluctuate, as does the rest of our plastic and unstable psychic life. This limitation ought not to depress us, but it ought to keep us in humility; and humility is the one grace which gives wings to the simplest prayer.

Finally, consider the ground we have traversed from the psychological point of view. What does it come to? Surely to a progressive abolition of concepts and reasonings, of realistic thought, a steady increase in the dominance of autistic thought or reverie—a bringing in of the marginal faculties, a widening of the arc of consciousness, and throwing open of fresh areas of the soul. The sanctions of prayer of this type must therefore depend on the following factors:

First, the extent in which we are willing to allow that spiritual forces are thus brought to play upon the deep-seated impulsive life, and so caused directly to influence the conduct which that impulsive life actuates. And here the tranquillizing, strengthening and finally transforming effect of regular and persevering meditation is well known.

Secondly, on our acknowledgment that the peculiar clairvoyance of the unconscious mind, which has already been demonstrated (though not explained) in other directions, extends also into the spiritual sphere; and that therefore recourse to it may be recourse to a veritable organ of knowledge. In the passive states of prayer, we give that unconscious mind the opportunity of presenting its results to the conscious reason and will. In saying this, of course, we merely seek to give a psychological account of what happens in these degrees; an account which leaves their religious meaning untouched. No experienced Christian will be willing to allow that in such prayer he merely explores his own buried resources. He is aware, at least in his deepest and most surrendered moments, of real contact with a real spiritual order, however dimly and mysteriously known: and from this contact he does receive renewal of assurance and of life. But without infringing the religious character of this experience or the proper reserves of the soul, I think we may and ought to seek some understanding of its psychology.

If, then, we look at the degrees of prayer as the great Christian specialists have usually taught them, in the light of this conception of the widening of the arc of consciousness, we perceive how their empirical methods receive the support of science. For (1) all these teachers begin with vocal prayer, the most direct and powerful instrument of suggestion, tuning up the psychic deeps for the activities we are to ask from them. (2) They proceed to meditation, bringing the imagination to bear on the soul's desired achievement, whether this be increase of virtue and grace, clearer realization of the objects of faith or conquest of special weakness and sin. By this exercise, the machinery of autistic thought is set going in the right direction, the great inner world of reverie is given over to the love of God, and that which might only have been dream becomes the strong instigator of act. Here the powers which commonly squander themselves on fantasy are rescued, and achieve their appropriate sublimation. (3) In the following degrees, of immediate acts and simplicity, sometimes grouped together as affective prayer, the unified or "recollected" self directs its whole impulsive longing in one direction. By its so-called "acts" and "aspirations" —brief suggestive phrases charged with feeling—it maintains this fruitful psychic state, gradually passing more and more completely into the prayer of simplicity or loving and silent attention to God. (4) In those temperamentally inclined to mystical prayer, the trained subliminal faculties may from time to time overflow, as it were, and dominate the conscious field. This is psychology's account of infused contemplation, as most simply experienced in the prayer of quiet. Nor need we consider such an account irreligious. We know in other departments of life that some of our greatest experiences and all our most fruitful intentions are undoubtedly prepared and matured in the subconscious deeps, and it is only their finished results that enter the conscious field. And this I believe to be true of the soul's deepest intercourse with God; abiding unbroken in the depths of personality, and thence overflowing as a transforming, strengthening and cleansing tide into the consciousness which is sufficiently pure, humble and attentive to receive it.

II

LIFE AS PRAYER[1]

"God is Spirit."—JOHN iv. 24, (*R.V.*, marg.)

" He is not far from each one of us: for in Him we live and move and have our being."—ACTS xvii.27–8 (*R.V.*)

I AM speaking to those who are bound together by the link of prayer, who seek communion with one another on an invisible plane and through a common surrender to an invisible love. And I wish to think with you a little about this binding link of prayer—this mysterious yet most real association of human spirits for the furthering of the purposes of God's creative Spirit.

What, then, is Prayer? In a most general sense, it is the intercourse of our little human souls with God. Therefore it includes all the work done by God Himself through, in, and with the souls which are self-given to Him in prayer. God is Spirit; we, His children, are little spiritual creatures. He is not far from each one of us. His life indwells each person in this room; and the communion of our separate lives with that fontal love and life is prayer. Prayer, then, is a purely spiritual activity; and its real doer is God Himself, the one inciter and mover of our souls.

So, how are we to begin to think about this mysterious, and yet very practical, work of prayer which we are all trying in some way or degree to do?

[1] An address given to a Fellowship of Prayer and issued by permission of the Author. Published by the Church of Scotland.

The first step, I suppose, is to try to reach a new and more vivid realization of the Holy Spirit of God—"God Himself as He is everywhere and in all things," as St. Thomas Aquinas says—ceaselessly at work upon our small and half-grown spirits; creating, illuminating, restoring and spiritualizing us. Now, God's creative and transforming action does not seem to work as something separate from the souls of men and women, but in and through those souls of men and women. "We are not," said Baron von Hügel, "to think of Spirit and spirit, God and the soul, as two separate entities. His Spirit works in closest association with ours."

A real man or woman of prayer, then, should be a live wire, a link between God's grace and the world that needs it. In so far as you have given your lives to God, you have offered yourselves, without conditions, as transmitters of His saving and enabling love: and the will and love, the emotional drive, which you thus consecrate to God's purposes, can do actual work on supernatural levels for those for whom you are called upon to pray. One human spirit can, by its prayer and love, touch and change another human spirit; it can take a soul and lift it into the atmosphere of God. This happens, and the fact that it happens is one of the most wonderful things in the Christian life. All your prayers, and far more than that, all your generous and loving desires, trials, sufferings, fatigues and renunciations—and of course there is no real life of prayer without all these—can avail for those persons and causes you seek to help. To all of them you are, or should be, agents or transmitters of the transforming, redeeming power of God; and the most real work you ever do should be that which you do secretly and alone.

The Christian fellowship, of which we are always hearing so much, is quite misunderstood, isn't it? if we think of it merely in terms of outward religious contact. For the real and vital communion between souls is invisible and spiritual—so deeply buried that we can think of it as existing unbroken below the changeful surface of daily life. External contact is at best only the outward sign of a far more profound inward grace—that mysterious interpenetration of all living souls, which is the secret of the Communion of Saints. And the whole possibility of intercessory prayer seems based on this truth of spiritual communion—the fact that we are *not* separate little units, but deeply interconnected—so that all we do, feel and endure has a secret effect, radiating far beyond ourselves. This is a thought that should help us when outward contacts are difficult or discouraging, or when circumstances limit our apparent "scope."

With some people this sympathetic contact with others actually reaches the conscious level. By their energy of love and pity they can enter and share the secret joys, needs, griefs and temptations of those with whom they are placed, can knowingly stand by and give them support, and literally bear the weight and suffering of their griefs, sins, and disease. We have all seen a little of this strange faculty in devoted mothers, devoted friends, and sometimes, too, in ministers of religion. In the saints it develops a marvellous vividness and power. That conscious stretching out of the soul may mean much suffering for those who can do it; but it also means a wonderful sense of close communion both with humanity and with God. Such people know for certain that when we pray we are never alone, but enter a vast spiritual society where genuine work is done. By their prayers they can deeply influence those with whom they are in contact. They can fight battles for them in secret, rescue, heal them and give them to God.

For the human soul is one of the instruments through which the "tranquil operations of His perpetual Providence" are performed. It is a living tool of the Holy Spirit which works in 'the world of prayer. All that it gains in its own secret life of adoration and communion it can and should give again to others in supernatural ways, thus becoming a real distributing centre of God's creative power. Drop by drop the enabling power of grace comes to us, and keeps on coming, out of the treasuries of the Eternal World—comes to us in our prayers and communions and in every opportunity of patience and sacrifice—and we can rely absolutely on that unfailing supply, provided that we spend it all again generously in redemptive work for the world, and especially for those to whom we are linked in prayer.

What we call "influence" is just the faint outward expression, the crude hint, of one of the ways in which the soul can thus work in prayer. Influence is due to the fact that every living personality stretches out tentacles, as it were, to touch and penetrate surrounding personalities; and suggests the immense power which we can thus exercise. Even influence, then, is enough to prove that human souls are truly open to and affected by the moulding action of each other's love and prayer—that they can take colour, and draw energy and peace, from the personalities among whom they are placed. So, no break with our regular experience is involved in the belief that the spiritual development of men is largely effected by God through those among whom He has placed them.

Each time you take a human soul with you into

your prayer, you accept from God a piece of spiritual work with all its implications and with all its cost—a cost which may mean for you spiritual exhaustion and darkness,and may even include vicarious suffering, the Cross. In offering yourselves on such levels of prayer for the sake of others, you are offering to take your part in the mysterious activities of the spiritual world; to share the saving work of Christ. Each soul thus given to your care brings a need which it is your job to meet, and an opportunity which will never be repeated, a duty that no one else can fulfil.

Of course it is in the saints that we see this love, and this intercessory power, acting on highest levels and effecting marvellous transformations. To learn what they did and do in their prayers is to realize what great untapped sources of power are all about us, ready for us to use if we will pay the price—lose our separate lives that we may find life. Consider such cases as those of St. Catherine of Siena, the young girl of the people whose spiritual transcendency transformed the ecclesiastical politics of her day, and who rescued countless sinners by her love and prayer: or the Curé d'Ars, the humble peasant priest who drew troubled souls from every corner of France and took on himself the burden of their sins; or Elizabeth Fry, going in the power of the Spirit to transform the awful life of the prisoners in Newgate Gaol. These, and countless others, make us realize how dreadfully shallow and careful, how ungenerous and untrusting our own little spiritual operations mostly are. Most of us do not really give our lives. At best we give a working day.

I am sure it was because the saints were so utterly uncalculating in their self-giving, cared for souls in such a divine way, and with such unmeasured love and eager acceptance of suffering, minded about people so much, that they did their great redeeming works of prayer. They show us that real intercession is not merely a petition but a piece of work, involving perfect, costly self-surrender to God for the work He wants done on other souls. Such great self-giving and great results may be their special privilege; still, they are showing us on a grand scale something which each cell of the Body of Christ has got to try to do on a small scale. They prove to us how closely and really all human spirits are connected—what we can do for one another if we only love enough—and how far-reaching is the power and responsibility of every Christian soul. We can only understand their experience by realizing that we are truly parts of a great spiritual organism. The Mystical Body of Christ is not an image, but a fact. We perpetually give and take from each other the indwelling Divine Life, and by our prayers, thoughts and actions affect all within our radius.

"All that you do," said the great Cardinal Mercier in one of his pastoral letters, "for good or evil, either benefits or damages the whole society of souls. The humblest of souls in the most obscure situation can, through the degree of virtue at which it lives and the work it is called to do, make its contribution to the general sanctification of the Church."

If that is literally true, then how much more is it true that the man or woman of prayer can apply all those things to the special needs of the persons or causes that God has placed in his care: and how fragmentary and superficial our outward Christian work will be, unless this interior sacrificial work is going on all the time.

Whenever man's love and man's religion transcends

the self-regarding stage and anchors itself on God, this sense that the soul is able to work and suffer for its fellows, and in some way share the eternal mystery of the Cross, seems to appear. I think none of us could deny that a strong redemptive and sacrificial element runs right through the best and deepest Christianity. The Christian religion is not just a beautiful system of ethics or a particular kind of belief about God. It is not only a devotion, however pure and loving, to the person of Christ. It does something to human nature which cannot be done in any other way. That sacrificial instinct so deeply planted in mankind, which finds such varied and strange expression as it follows the upward path of evolution—this it is which triumphs in the real intercessory life. Self-offering, loving, unconditional and courageous, is therefore the first requirement of true intercessory prayer. The interceding soul must be willing to go with our Lord to Gethsemane and Calvary, and share with Him the crushing weight of the world's sin, disorder, disease.

That is a tremendous model to set before ourselves, isn't it? But, at any rate, it is a model that helps us most when we need it most. Just because it appeals to what is most heroic in us, it makes us glad and anxious to do such bits of this mysterious divine work as may fall to our share, whatever strain and renunciation they may require. We are here the assistants of that Good Shepherd who gives His life for the sheep.

Now, if we are thus to offer ourselves for and in those sick and helpless sheep, we shall not do it only by deliberately religious deeds and thoughts; for no one, without unhealthy strain, can keep all his deeds and thoughts on the religious level all the time. We shall do it as human beings as well as spiritual beings. That is, by more and more giving spiritual and intercessory value to *all* the acts and intentions of life, however homely, practical and simple; lifting that whole life, visible and invisible, on to the sacramental plane, turning it into prayer. As every thought and act of all its members really affects the whole spiritual society, so every thought and act of the intercessor can be entinctured with the special grace of his vocation; and really and secretly radiate to affect all those lives with which God has closely bound up his soul.

Therefore physical, mental and spiritual labour, with all the successes and failures, the difficulties, sufferings, demands on patience and humility that go with each kind, can all become the vehicles of our spiritual effectiveness; if every bit is given, by intention, for the good of those who are in our prayer. These things, which can all be the means of raising us towards God, must be the means of raising other souls at the same time. For the real worth of intercessions does not consist in the specific things we ask for or obtain, but in the channel offered by our love and sacrifice to the creative and redeeming love and will of God. We open a fresh path to His Spirit; make straight the way along which He reaches a needy soul, a struggling movement, or a desolate corner of life.

Perhaps the contact will be made through some act of loving service on our part. Perhaps it will be our disciplined spirit of joy and peace which reaches out to those who most deeply need that inner tranquillity. Perhaps the contact will not be made outwardly at all, but secretly in the world of prayer. However it may be made, it is essential to realize that here it is our privilege to minister the supernatural—

God, in His richness and wonder; that He is coming through us to other souls in the way in which they can bear it best. The steadfast pressure of the Divine Energy and Love, felt at different levels and in different ways right through creation, is finding in us a special path of discharge.

Surely we need not be surprised if all this costs us a good deal; for real spiritual work taxes to the utmost the limited powers of the natural creature. It is using them on a fresh level, subjecting them to fresh strains. And this means that our preparation for it, if we are beginners, our maintenance in a fit condition for it if we are mature, is an important part of our religious life. It will not be managed merely by suitable reading, church attendance, prayer circles or anything of that kind; but only by faithful personal attention to God, constant and adoring recourse to Him, confident humble communion with Him. And the upkeep of this life-giving contact with the Eternal World, this secret intercourse with the living Christ, is a primary duty which we owe to those for whom we pray. The loving, enraptured vision of God, the limitless self-forgetful confidence in God, the generous desire to give without stint for His purposes—these are the sources of those intercessions which have power.

What quality, then, is it in us that can thus become the agent of the Divine creativity? Not our intellects, however brilliant; not our faith, however clear and correct; not our active works, however zealous. We may lack all these; and yet through us God's work may be done.

There is ultimately only one thing in us that can and will be used by God to carry His love and power from soul to soul, and that is the mysterious thing we call a consecrated personality. This is surely the lesson of the Incarnation—a lesson repeated again and again in the history of the Church. Not what Christ did and said, but what He was and is, guarantees God to man, and brings God's power to man. And similarly, on our own tiny scale, not what we say or do, but what we are, provides the medium through which God reaches those to whom we are sent. Thus we come back again, don't we? to the point at which we began; that the first duty of the intercessor is communion with that Spirit in Whom our being is. Thus only we build up in ourselves a strong and pure spiritual life; thus we grow, sanctify ourselves for the sake of our work. It is for this work that we must keep the sense of wide horizons; our prayers will not escape religious pettiness unless we can do this. And it is for this that we must have spiritual food and fresh air, and receive in prayer the supernatural sunshine; not so much for the sake of its consoling warmth and light, as for the powerful but invisible chemical rays which give us spiritual vitality. We must keep ourselves sensitive to the Eternal, delicately responsive to God.

This is a thing, we know, which no human creature can achieve by its own anxious efforts. It is given from beyond ourselves; but given to those who look steadily in the right direction, and accept the inward discipline which is the only preparation of peace. Thus adoring, self-oblivious vision, confident and unbroken interior communion with God, secret and tranquil renunciation, remain our first duties; for these are the real source and support of the devoted energies of the true intercessor, and of all those who offer themselves for the furtherance of God's work in the world of prayer.

III

WORSHIP[1]

I AM going to speak this afternoon on a subject which, it seems to me, ought to be of vital interest to students of religion and still more, to those who are trying to *live* religion: Worship. Theology deals with the material of religion; the Fact of God and His revelation to men. Worship is religion in action; man's total response to that God who is the subject of theology. So here we have those two complementary aspects of man's religious life which medieval symbolism expressed when it placed near God the cherubim, who were the spirits of divine knowledge; and nearer still the seraphim, who were the spirits of adoring love.

Now I may as well confess at once that "worship" is not a word I like very much: partly because it seems to put man's attitude and man's doings too much in the foreground of religion—partly because it does not seem quite good enough, quite strong enough, to describe the relation in which the human soul should stand and the praise it should offer to the unsearchable majesty and loveliness of God. However, there the word is, and we seem almost obliged to use it. What then ought worship to mean to us? What should its essence be?

I think it should cover that whole element in our life which is directed towards God the Transcendent,

[1] A lecture given at the Annual Meeting of the Guild of the Epiphany, Stationers' Hall, January 12th, 1929. Published by A. R. Mowbray & Co. Ltd.

and done simply and solely for God the Transcendent. Not because of its usefulness, not because we want something, not because it does us any good; but solely *for Him*. "Worship," which after all only means honour, gives rather a frosty account of this great human impulse; in which, as a matter of fact, there is always an element of adoring love.

Such a definition as this of course extends our idea of worship far beyond what are usually called religious exercises. But I think we grasp the meaning and the essential character of those religious exercises —and especially of public worship—much better if we look upon them as being the condensed, dramatic, though very imperfect expressions of the instinct of worship; that adoring attitude over against Transcendental Reality which is implanted in the human soul. It is an instinct that finds expression not only in our devotional, but also in our æsthetic life. The inspiration òf the painter, the musician and the poet, and often that of the scientist and explorer too, contains a genuine element of worship. All that is best in these great human activities is not done for our own sakes; it points right away from us, to something we humbly seek and half-ignorantly adore. It is offered at the shrine of a beauty or a wisdom that lies beyond the world.

Regarded in this way, worship is the great spiritual action of mankind; that for which he has been made. It is the homage paid by the soul to its origin. The whole duty of man, said St. Ignatius, is to "praise, reverence and serve God our Lord"—that is our contribution to the purpose of the universe. In it we transcend the ordinary visible world of time—get, as the mystics say, beyond Then and Now—and join with the whole Communion of Saints, the living and

E

the dead, in reverent adoring delight in God. Each time we "go to church" we ought in spirit to be entering that eternal world. A church is a little place fenced off from the distracting bustle of existence, and which is filled or should be filled with an atmosphere and with suggestions that make it easier for those who go there to realize the worshipping life. If we were pure spirits, of course, we should not need such concessions to our weakness; but being what we are, creatures of the borderland, we need them very much indeed. We need surroundings which encourage us to attend to God. It is through such steadfast attention that men learn to know Him: for we can only know in a real sense that which we love, gaze at, admire and enjoy, and this is worship. Worship is not therefore getting information about God; though learning from those who know more about Him than we do may help us to worship better. It is not telling Him our sins and asking for forgiveness— though once the human creature begins to grasp what worship is, it is driven to confess its rebellions, imperfections and nothingness and ask for that restoring energy we call grace. Nor is it recommending to His notice the persons and causes which happen to interest us. Exhortation, confession, intercession, all have their place in man's religious life; but they are something less than worship. Worship is the little human spirit's humble adoring acknowledgment of the measureless glory of God, the only Reality—the Perfect, the Unchanging, the entirely Free.

"What can I say, my God, my Holy Joy?" says St. Augustine, "What can any man say when he speaks of Thee?" *That* is the spirit of worship.

Because we are social creatures, this acknowledgment of God must be made by us in corporate as well as individual ways. Human beings have developed through acting together; and unless they do so, a part of their nature fails to expand. Thus the secret acts of praise, the hidden communion with God, which are the essence of private devotion, can never be enough for full Christian worship. The homage offered by the human soul to God, the Father of all, must have its social and visible embodiment. Further, because men are creatures of sense as well as spirit, of body as well as soul, we must bring our senses and our bodies in, and let them play their part in the worshipping act. Thus Quaker silence, in itself most precious, is not really enough for full Christian worship. It is based on a virtual antithesis between body and soul, outward and inward, which is bad psychology; and also I venture to think, bad theology. Eye and ear—even touch, taste and smell—are veritable channels through which our sense-conditioned spirits can receive messages from God and respond to Him.

It is true that at bottom worship is a spiritual activity; but we are not pure spirits, and therefore we cannot expect to do it in purely spiritual ways. That is the lesson of the Incarnation. Thus liturgies, music, symbols, sacraments, devotional attitudes and acts have their rightful part to play in the worshipping life; and it is both shallow and arrogant to reject them *en masse* and assume that there is something particularly religious in leaving out the senses when we turn to God. Through such use of the senses man can receive powerful religious suggestions, and by their help can impregnate an ever wider area of his life and consciousness with the spirit of adoration. If music is something that may awaken the awed awareness of the Holy, if pictures can tell us secrets that are beyond speech, if food and water, fragrance and lights, all bear with them a memory of sacred use—then the ordinary deeds of secular life will become more and more woven into the seamless robe that veils the Glory of God. But this will not happen unless the sacramental principle—the principle of the spiritual significance of visible deeds and things—has a definite expression in our organized religious life.

When we look at the essential character of any of our experiences, what do we find there? We find, do we not, three distinct factors? First oneself, the consciously experiencing person. Then, that which we experience; which certainly is not just ourselves, but something else—something over against us. And then, the surrounding world, or society, in which we are placed, within which the experience happens and from which we can never quite cut ourselves free. That is, subject, object and environment are concerned in all the activities and experiences of men; in fact, we had better say, of all living things. And when we come to religious or spiritual experience, these three factors stand out with great clearness. Everything that matters about man's communion with God and response to God can be placed in one of those three categories: and it is under those three heads that I now propose to consider the essentials of worship.

(1) We will put first—what is so often put last in discussions of religious experience—God, who is the object of worship; not man, the subject who worships Him. God the only Reality, however we may apprehend Him—whether in a very simple or very theological way matters little; as in either event it is sure

to be an inadequate way. It is His actuality, His intensity of love, life and power over against men's souls, and the loving adoration which He evokes from those souls—at first very blind, dim and blundering, but coming ever into greater clearness with the progress of the race—which is the *stuff* of the worshipping life. The object of that life is not our moral or even spiritual betterment. The Object in its absolute perfection and beauty shines unchanged; whether men are religious or irreligious, good or bad. "He is all and doth all if thou couldst but see Him," said one of the mystics—there stating the central truth of all theism. Deep down in men's souls is a persistent sense that this is true: and when this sense rises up into consciousness, we are moved by love and worship for the Home and Father of our souls. So the first essential of true worship is that which is given us so wonderfully in the vision of Isaiah—the Glory of the Lord must fill the temple. This is equally true whether God be sought alone on the mountain, or in the corporate silence of a Quaker meeting, or under the veils of sacramental devotion. Every time, the only thing that matters is the unchanging Glory of God. Man has to tune in to that universal voice of adoration which says all the time—whether we notice it or not—Holy, holy, holy, Lord God of hosts! Heaven and earth are full of Thy Glory: Glory be to Thee, O Lord most High! The *Sanctus* is the classic norm of all human worship. This consideration at once makes us feel rather low about the average tone of corporate religion, does it not? About the view of worship which I once saw perfectly expressed in an advertisement for a curate—"no surplice work except on Sundays."

A soul which is worshipping God is acknowledging

—even though it may not be able to feel, which is quite a different thing—the implications of the *Sanctus*: acknowledging that God is all that matters; and that it is His glory which makes anything else worth while. This note of solemn yet joyous adoration, which obliterates all thoughts of self, ought then to be the first point, both in public worship and in the private devotional life which supports that public worship and makes it real. For this is the Church's acknowledgment that the First Commandment does come first: a fact that most modern presentations of Christianity scandalously neglect. The historic liturgies of the Christian Church, whether Latin, Anglican or Orthodox, constantly emphasize this principle. If we could only forget how familiar we are with our own English version of that liturgy, and look at it with the freshness with which we look at a great work of art—and it is a great work of art—we should realize this. See how all the great Christian rituals have instinctively seized and held on to the very words of Isaiah's seraphim as the one essential prelude to the most solemn act of Christian devotion —the Eucharist. See how persistent, all through the ancient daily offices from which our Morning and Evening Prayer are drawn, is the emphasis on God's Being, rather than on man's needs. The Psalms—the greater number of which are poems praising God, exalting His greatness and mercy, His cherishing care, over against the littleness of men, or meditating on some aspect of His Nature—these are to be the regular daily food of the worshipping soul.

O God, Thou art my God: early will I seek Thee.
Unto Thee lift I up mine eyes, O Thou that dwellest in the Heavens!

For Thou, O Lord God, art the thing that I long for!
O Lord our Governor, how excellent is Thy name in
    all the world!

Then the daily use of the Canticles and *Venite*:

Come! let us *sing* unto the Lord! Let us show our-
    selves glad in Him with psalms!
My soul doth magnify the Lord: and my spirit hath
    rejoiced . . .

What a refreshing note of delight! Directly we begin
to take those words quite literally, to feel self-
oblivious gladness in the reality and beauty of God
for His own sake, we have begun to know something
about worship.

Now we cannot be glad about something we do not
know: and the human mind left to itself is wholly
unable to know God. Therefore it is the self-giving
of that Infinite God to us, His showing of Himself to
us, His prevenient action in theological terms, which
is the true cause of the impulse to worship that
springs up in men's hearts. The story of man's
religious life is throughout a story of God's movement to man, and man's response. Without that
initial self-revelation of God, that manifestation out
of the deep mysteries which surround us, of a cherishing, merciful love, a saving energy, an other-worldly
beauty that cuts right across the apparent sin and
misery of the world—without this, men could never
have known that God was adorable. They could not
feel awe and love, and the longing to prostrate themselves before Him. The fact that the most spiritual
men in all religions have felt this so intensely witnesses—does it not?—to the secret action of the
Spirit, teaching human beings, in the way in which

they can receive it, to love God with heart, mind and strength. As Von Hügel put it, He "secretly initiates what He openly crowns."

Some realization of that tremendous spiritual truth is an essential of all real worship. And surely the entrancing, touching beauty of the Christian revelation consists very largely in the way in which it declares to us this coming down of the Infinite God into the human arena; first self-disclosed through personality, and then with an even more complete and so more royal self-abasement, self-given in the sacraments through natural things. When we set these considerations against the vast background of the Universe, it is not surprising that they have made religious souls "lose themselves in wondering at Him." So the due presentation of God in public institutional worship will include not only such great expressions of adoring joy in His Reality as the Psalms, the Canticles, the Sanctus give us; but the deeper and more homely thoughts and feelings evoked by the Incarnation, and its continuance in the great Christian sacraments, which turn the majestic phrases of the Creed into an act of praise. The celebration of the Christian year from Advent to Whitsuntide, the tendency to surround the Eucharist with greater dignity and outward beauty, all enlarge and enrich the field within which this Spirit of Worship can find its opportunities of expression.

(2) This brings us to the second aspect of our subject: the ways in which this self-oblivious, non-utilitarian adoration of God for His own sake ought to be expressed; the balance that should be kept in it. Look again at the statement with which we began— the three factors ever present in our experience;

subject, object, environment. Here they are of course God, the unchanging Object; then our human religious environment—the Church, with its tradition and cultus; and then our own changing, growing human spirits, the subjects who are trying to worship God. And at once that gives us certain elements on which to build our framework. It gives us praise, adoration, as the prime duty, the Opus Dei, the pre-eminent work of God, as St. Benedict called it—and then the great Christian tradition which has nurtured us, and provides us with a common language, common material, common symbols, with which this work of God, this spiritual action, is to be done. And finally our own souls, the society of human beings, partly physical and partly spiritual creatures, whose minds and senses can only act in certain ways. We are not angels, and we are not yet living under purely spiritual conditions. We are just a society of human creatures conditioned by and greatly depending on history; creatures anchored to this planet, and with a good deal of the animal about us still. It is more humble and more sensible to remember these facts, in religion as elsewhere, than to try to escape from them. And they mean that, in expressing our religion, in worshipping that Eternal Spirit from whom those very conditions come, and whose action on our souls reaches us through history and through the senses, men must keep in close touch with history; and not be afraid to acknowledge that the spiritual world comes to them through eyes, ears and touch, as well as in what we like to call "purely spiritual" ways.

First, History. We all realize that as Christians we belong to a historical religion. We are not pious individualists, but part of a historical Church. It is literally true that we are treading where the saints have trod. Yet some of the demands that are made in the name of liturgical reform and the claims put forward in the name of religious experience seem to ignore this great truth, showing a quite exaggerated respect for the present moment and its special notions, and individuals and their special feelings and ideas. Real, fully corporate worship, genuine institutional religion, rests on the solidarity of the whole Christian family—the blessed company of *all* faithful people past and present, living and dead, from St. Peter and St. Paul to the last baptized baby. Every time we join in that worship we are joining with the whole Communion of Saints; who are just as real and living as we are—probably in the deepest sense much more living and real. *They* form part of that environment in which we worship; and our services ought to have in them a sufficient historical element to remind us of this fact. A preservation of historic continuity—something that ensures remembrance of our unbroken fellowship with the little company in the Upper Room, that reminds us of those spiritual ancestors on whose rich inheritance we, very largely, live—is essential to the corporate character of Christian worship. That means liturgy, a devotional matrix within which the love, praise, penitence and needs of the worshipper can be expressed. The complaints we sometimes hear on this subject, about the formal and unreal character of our services, archaic language, and so forth, are largely due to our want of historical imagination—which might surely be roused to enthusiasm by that wonderful device whereby as it were we transcend the time-process and re-enter the past, to find it living and glowing with a devotional fire which ought to shame us. In our corporate worship we stand again with the awe-

struck Isaiah in the Temple and hear the ceaseless cry
of the seraphim. We join with the long line of Hebrew
and Christian saints in using that poetry of the
Psalms which was so often on our Lord's lips. We
confess that like lost sheep we err and stray from a
flock that is always one. We perform the same
humble and sacred acts that have been handed down
to us by the long succession of lovers of Christ. We
can hear again in their primitive freshness the
mysterious story of the Gospel, or the letters of St.
Paul; can discover that the joy of the first Christians
was just the same joy as our own ought to be, because
based on an experience that continues still; and that
we are being led to an identical goal—God, the unchanging country of the soul.

"My soul doth magnify the Lord: and my spirit
hath rejoiced in God my Saviour."

Look deeply into those words, place them against
the background of the universe; and you will see that
with all our modern thought, our modern outlook, we
have not really got beyond that. The pure essence
of the relationship between the Infinite God and the
human soul is there. Our mistake is, that we take it
all too much on the surface, too much by rote; and
never dig for its hidden and immortal gold. Yet even
so, how raw and thin a religious experience would be
which cut itself off from this long liturgical history,
refused all this culture, these gifts of the past. Such
an independence of tradition might be possible in a
spiritual genius. But it would mean hopeless im-
poverishment for the average soul; which, like the
average baby, depends for food, shelter and support
on the social life into which it is born, and only
acquires tone and value through its incorporation in
the common life.

And this brings us to the third essential factor of worship. We see that it must be concentrated upon its supreme Object—God, in His adorableness. It must be subdued to its environment, human history and human conditions; must keep in touch with the average human mind and its limitations, accept and use—humbly but not slavishly—all that is given to it by the tradition and corporate life of the Church. It has got to strike a careful balance between the Eternal and the Historical: and between the living freshness of the present moment and a reverent use of the treasures of the past.

Last, what are the relations in which it stands to the subject—the worshipping individual—you and me? Must not this great social activity, this adoring act of the Christian family life, directed to God in and for Himself, also do something for each worshipping soul? And must not each separate worshipping soul also do something for it? Surely both must be true. For, first of all, no activity of our life leaves us quite as it found us. It always has some reflex effect; indeed, our physical and mental development is largely effected by the things we deliberately do, and especially by the things we do together. The corporate atmosphere, where it is favourable, stimulates and refreshes our own languid religious life, lifts us above our common level; so that we come away from a great act of worship feeling as if we have breathed great draughts of mountain air. So too the pressure of suggestion, the steady and disciplined use of common forms, will mould and educate, give its particular form, to our personal spiritual life. We have all had experience of that, so I need not enlarge on it. Hence, though we must never recommend corporate worship for utilitarian reasons—because it does us good—as a matter of fact it *does* do us good.

But there is another side to this. We in our turn can and should do *it* good. The force, depth and realness of the common worship depends very largely on the sincerity and devotedness of the individuals taking part in it. People who talk contemptuously about "empty forms" forget that empty things can always be filled, and that it is up to them to do it. The silliest hymn and most formal prayer can be made a great act of worship; if those who use it have worshipping instead of critical hearts. The old saint to whom men came on his deathbed, asking how they could restore the services of the Church, and who replied to each questioner like a minute gun, "Love God! Love God!" had the root of the matter in him.

Thus the private preparation of our own souls for the public worship of God, by our prayers and thoughts and the discipline of our love, is a duty we owe to the whole mystical body of which we are cells —to the whole Communion of Saints. Public worship is an activity in which we develop a group consciousness and apply that group consciousness to religious ends. The words and forms we use are designed to support and nourish this. But ultimately this group-action, like all kinds of social life, depends on the health and energy of each unit. Here each individual has a definite responsibility; and only in so far as he fulfils that can he expect to receive all that this common devotional life has to give.

What has it to give? Perhaps the greatest of the things which the discipline of corporate worship does for those who submit to its influence is that it delivers them from that cramping tendency to self-occupation by which nearly all human beings—and especially pious human beings—are beset: *my* soul, *my* spiritual life, *my* sins, *my* problems, *my* communion with God. All true and important facts no doubt; but facts that get on best, like many hardy annuals, if well thinned out in the first instance and then left to themselves. All that sort of thing is drowned in a great common act of praise and joy; a common act of communion and self-dedication. Many a congregation when it assembles in church must look to the angels like a muddy puddly shore at low tide; littered with every kind of rubbish and odds and ends—a distressing sort of spectacle. And then the tide of worship comes in, and it's all gone: the dead sea-urchins and jelly-fish, the paper and the empty tins and nameless bits of rubbish. The cleansing sea flows over the whole lot. So we are released from a narrow selfish outlook on the universe by a common act of worship. Our little human affairs are reduced to their proper proportion when seen over against the spaceless Majesty and Beauty of God. All other things apart, is it not a priceless privilege to be able to resort to an experience wherein those who come with good will can be sure of getting that?

You remember how Emerson says that coming out one starry night from some meeting where he had been passionately absorbed in defending his own ideas and affairs, struggling for his own point of view, the great stars looking down seemed to say to him, "Why so hot, little man? Why so hot?" So we come, with our little worries and preoccupations, our often very petty religious preferences, into the noble atmosphere of worship—so much greater than ourselves—so much greater than this one small planet—

with Angels and Archangels and with all the company of Heaven lauding and magnifying that one glorious Name—and we too recover proportion, and with proportion peace. Those mighty realities into whose presence worship brings us seem to say to us, "Why so hot, little man? Why so hot?" We are eternalized; our minds are lifted to the Unchanging. Two or three are gathered together, throw into the common stock their faith and devotion; and the Holy is found in their midst. And by this brief experience we receive something which helps us in our turn to perform our share of the Christian duty of manifesting that Unchanging Perfection in the world of time. Therefore, though religious worship is never to be recommended because of its result on ourselves, we can test its reality and quality most surely by those results.

Look again at Isaiah. What did the mighty act of worship into which he was introduced do for him? First of all, taught him humility—that is to say, proportion. It brought him down with a run. Face to face with the Glory of God, all that *he* was or wanted went for nothing. "Woe is me! because I am a man of unclean lips, and I dwell in the midst of a people of unclean lips!" In the light of perfect holiness he began to see things as they are, get the proportions of existence right. If worship blends with joy this humble sense of nothingness, we may hope it is on the right path. Within such a corporate act of adoration, confession and supplication will inevitably have their place. Perhaps the Prayer of Humble Access is the most beautiful and balanced expression in our liturgy of this complete yet confident self-abasement before God.

And last: it is a very significant part of the story of Isaiah's vision that his awe, penitence and purification are not presented as ends in themselves. The Lord reveals His splendour to Isaiah, calls him to worship, gives him purifying and enabling grace, because the completion of this process shall be his free, spontaneous dedication to the purposes of God. "Send me." He would not have said that, unless his eyes had first been opened to the glory. So, if the first point of worship is the creature's adoration of God, the second is that same little creature's total self-offering—total willing capitulation—to that God: in other words his *Sacrifice*. Adoration and sacrifice, in one form or another, are the responses of the soul to the attraction of God: the essential notes of the worship man is called and privileged to pay.

"Here we offer and present unto thee, O Lord, ourselves, our souls and bodies, to be a reasonable, holy, and lively sacrifice unto thee!"

We can hardly surround with too much beauty and dignity this supreme act of the soul; for here man passes from the worshipping act to the worshipping life.

"What ask I of thee more," says à Kempis, "but that thou study to resign thyself to me entirely? What thing soever thou givest me else I care not for. For I demand not thy gifts but only thyself."

Worship is the response of humanity to that wonderful demand.

IV

THOUGHTS ON PRAYER AND THE DIVINE IMMANENCE[1]

I

SENATOR MARCONI has lately said in an interview that the discovery and development of wireless may yet give us a scientific basis for prayer—the most mysterious perhaps of all man's powers and activities. Sir James Jeans suggests a more profound analogy when he tells us in *The Mysterious Universe* that the radiation of every electron composing the physical cosmos is bounded only by the limits of that cosmos. Thus the outpouring and self-giving energies of one such electron can fill all space; and during our whole lives we are receiving and are conditioned by the radiations and influence of countless worlds and their unimaginable constituents, falling on us, changing us, maintaining us. That is an impressive allegory of the universe of spirit, and the unseen forces by which it is maintained, and gains in significance when we consider how spendthrift, powerful, and costly is the spiritual radiation of the saints. But it is an allegory which seems to imply a view of prayer that regards it as a purely human and largely a utilitarian activity; a force which man directs to God; or which, by a sort of holy telepathy, he can exert by his own choice and cost as towards his fellow-men. Yet we cannot on this basis construct such a wide and rich doctrine of Christian prayer as shall find a place for its most far-reaching characters

[1] *Expository Times*, June 1931.

and developments. Any study of it which conceives it mainly, so to speak, as the action of discrete spiritual individuals, surely misses its central truth; namely, the solidarity of that total and supernatural action which is brought into existence by the Divine energy and exerted by God through and in the corporate activity of all praying souls.

For what, after all, is prayer? It is a mutual act, a communion of the created spirit with Uncreated Spirit: of the human self, immersed in contingency and succession, with the all-penetrating God who yet transcends contingency and succession—in whom, as St. Augustine said, "are all moments of time." It is therefore the religious act *par excellence*; and rightly understood, should give us a clue to all that religion means in the life of man. "We know in general," says Grou, "that prayer is a religious act; but when it comes to praying, we easily lose sight of the fact that it is a supernatural act, which is consequently beyond our power, and which we cannot properly perform without the inspiration and help of grace." The initiative then, in all genuine prayer, is not human but Divine. It is a work of prevenience. And next, I think, we must add that this communion of spirit with Spirit to which we are mysteriously urged, and which more and more dominates those lives that are becoming sensitive to God, is purposive. It always looks beyond itself to some further creative goal—great or small, general or particular, remote or immediate—to be achieved by this collaboration of Divine and human will and desire. If we give a sufficiently wide and deep content to our terms, this will be found on analysis to be true even of the most apparently passive and formless prayer of contemplation, which seems to the praying soul to be no

more than the expression of its own thirst for surrender, and merely to place it at the disposal of God.
For since the ultimate goal of the immanent Divine
Will must be the supernaturalization of all life, and
prayer is a sovereign means through which the Divine
Immanence works, we cannot deny the purposive
nature of such passive and generalized prayer. It is
indeed always declared by the mystics to have profound effects, which are not limited by its transforming action on personality. They regard it as the
medium of an actual conveyance of life, and hence
the direct cause of their powers. "This prayer,
stripped of image and apperception, idle in appearance and yet so active, is," says Grou again, "the
adoration truly worthy of God, wherein the soul
unites herself to Him in her ground; the created
intelligence to Uncreated Intelligence, without the
intervention of imagination or reasoning or anything
else but a very simple attention of the mind and an
equally simple application of the will."

Prayer, then, in the most general sense, is from the
Divine side purposive. Its creative goal, however,
may be concerned with almost any level or aspect of
physical or spiritual life; for the prayer of a wide-
open and surrendered human spirit appears to be a
major channel for the free action of that Spirit of
God with whom this soul is "united in her ground."
Thus it seems certain that the energy of prayer can
avail for the actual modifying of circumstance; and
that its currents form an important constituent of
that invisible web which moulds and conditions
human life. It may open a channel along which
power, healing or enlightenment goes to those who
need it, as the watering-can provides the channel
along which water goes to the thirsty plant. Or the

object achieved may be, as we say, "directly spiritual"; the gradual purifying and strengthening and final sublimation of the praying soul or of some other particular soul. In all such cases, though much remains mysterious, the connection between prayer and result appears as the connection of genuine cause and effect. We are plainly in the presence of that which Elisabeth Leseur called "a high and fruitful form of action, the more secure that it is secret." On the other hand, the prayer may seem to have no specified aim; and this is specially true of its more developed forms. As spiritual writers say, its energies may simply be "given to God." Thus it may do a work which remains for ever unknown to the praying soul; contributing to the good of the whole universe of spirits, the conquest of evil, the promotion of the Kingdom, the increased energy of holiness. Such general and sacrificial prayer has always formed part of the interior life of the saints, and is an enduring strand in the corporate work of the Church. When St. Teresa founded the Discalced Carmelites, it was not to promote the culture of individual souls, but in order that the corporate hidden prayer of these communities might generate power, combating in some degree the wickedness she saw in the world. It was of this aspect of prayer that Cardinal Mercier spoke, when he said in one of his pastorals, "Through an ever closer adherence to the Holy Spirit in the sanctuary of your soul, you can, from within your home circle, the heart of your country, the boundary of your parish, overpass all earthly frontiers and . . . intensify and extend the Kingdom of Love."

For genuine prayer in all its degrees, from the most naïve to the most transcendental, opens up human personality to the all-penetrating Divine activity. Progress in prayer, whatever its apparent form, consists in the development of this its essential character. It places our souls at the disposal of immanent Spirit. In other words, it promotes abandonment to God; and this in order that the soul's separate activity may more and more be invaded, transfigured, and at last superseded by the unmeasured Divine action. In Pauline language, maturity of soul is to be gauged by the extent in which the Spirit "prays in us." Such deductions from observed experience can only be made humbly and tentatively; for one factor, God, is largely unknown to us, and the other, the soul, only in a subjective way. But we may say without impropriety that prayer—first incited by God's prevenient action, and then used by Him for His creative purpose—is to be regarded from man's side as a movement out towards absolute action, and from God's side as one of the ways in which the Divine Immanence works.

II

It follows from all this that there can be no valid and realistic doctrine of prayer which does not rest on and involve a doctrine of God: and conversely that no doctrine of God is adequate which does not take account, and even very great account, of the findings of the life of prayer. We cannot separate spiritual practice and spiritual belief without reducing the first to a dependence on our fluctuating feeling-states, and the second to a series of "agreed propositions." In prayer the soul comes nearest the expression of absolute love: in belief it ascends by means of symbols towards absolute truth. *Lex orandi lex credendi* is true then, perhaps in a far more actual sense than those who first made that axiom supposed. On the one hand the life of prayer is at least as much an established fact in the human world as the life of creative art or philosophic thought. It arises and develops wherever there is a living sense of God. Therefore its witness to reality should be accorded the respectful attention due to any "real existent." The attempts of naturalistic psychology to explain it on subjective lines break down before any honest and persistent study of its real character and achievements. So, too, all efforts to account for its existence by reference to the outlook and habits of primitive man evade the real issue, and merely describe the puppy without reference to the functions of the dog. For prayer is rooted in ontology. It is an appeal from the successive to the Abiding, without which succession has no meaning at all. It is a genuine communion with Reality, or nothing. This communion may be in its beginnings crude and childish; directed towards such signs and images as mediate the Transcendent to the awakening soul. But even so, it points beyond the natural scene to the concrete reality and independence of God, His attraction, His free and intimate working in human life: and marks the first stirrings of the creaturely sense. Thus the very existence of the life of prayer—adoration, communion, impetration, however naïve their primitive embodiments—requires for its explanation the immanent presence and self-disclosure of this real and actual God, and cannot be accounted for in terms of human or natural process.

Moreover, prayer, and especially the result of prayer, bears its own witness to the character of this Immanent God; and corrects the modern emphasis on visible Nature as the capital scene of His self-disclosure to man. For it leads the self into a level of life wholly other than that of Nature; and shows it the rich and mysterious web of existence in spiritual regard. And though this vision is far too great for us, and produces by its very radiance the obscurities of faith, still these humbling disclosures which awe and delight us, these glimpses of the dark mystery of God, do effect first a purification and then an undreamed expansion and enlightenment of the psyche; making it more supple to the Divine action, more amenable to the creative pressure of the Divine life. By that inward growth which has been codified as the "ascending degrees of prayer," the human self does more and more transcend the physical. It enters more and more into a richer and deeper knowledge of God, a sense of the profoundly purposive character that inheres in all the movements of the Spirit; whether realized through circumstances, or obscurely felt in the soul. So that it comes at last to the state which, says St. John of the Cross, consists simply in this, that "the soul must now learn to receive, to let Another act in her."

This means that the knowledge of Divine Immanence which grows with the deepening of man's prayer is also the knowledge of a Divine Otherness. Hence the constantly heard modern invitation to seek and find God in Nature—that is to say, in the physical scene, or rather our ever-changing and often bewildered apprehension of that physical scene—may result in actual damage to the deepest interests of religion, if it is allowed to obscure the primacy of those revelations of reality which are made only in the deeps of that communion wherein the spirit "seeks God in her ground." "The closer a soul approaches God by love," says Maritain, "the simpler grows the gaze of her intelligence, and the clearer her vision." And this loving approach to God Himself, for Himself and for none of His works, is of the very essence of prayer.

This intimate connection between vision and love is borne out by experience: as indeed we must expect, if the Christian doctrine of the Holy Spirit—the indwelling of the creature by the Godhead under its attribute of purposive love—be true. The mind and soul of a mature man of prayer have simplified their gaze, and deepened and broadened their correspondences with Reality; and the result is seen in a peculiar confidence in the universe, a profound and peaceful acceptance of experience in its wholeness and not only in purely religious regard. Such a soul, though it may and commonly does remain inarticulate as regards its deepest findings, knows existence, is aware of the mysterious movements and pressure of the Spirit, in a way others do not. Because of its humble and disciplined communion with that immanent Spirit, it has achieved a flexibility which can move to and fro between the inward and the outward finding in both in the most actual sense the presence of a living, acting God. It is this loving discernment of Reality through and in prayer, this experience, which is meant by the phrase "mystical theology" as employed by the great Christian masters of the spiritual life. And dogmatic theology, too, is necessarily concerned with Truth as seen from this angle; from within the house of prayer, and in the state of prayer. For here, within the house, though the lighting is dim, and much that we vaguely perceive is beyond our comprehension, we do at least realize the use of those pipes and chimney-pots which looked so queer and disconcerting from outside. Our difficulty in giving living content to our religious formulas, the dreadful sense of unreality which clings to many of the definitions of faith, arise very largely from the fact that we are thus viewing from the outside that which can only disclose its meaning when seen from the inside. For only in prayer, and in that state of soul which its practice tends to produce in us, can we know in any genuine sense the penetrating energy, the glowing splendour, the intimate yet unearthly pressure of that Divine Immanence which is the conditioning fact of personal religion. And to know this is to part company for ever from the dilute and sentimental immanentisms of naturalistic piety.

Thus it becomes clear that the theology of prayer is closely bound up with the theology of the Holy Spirit. Indeed, it is important to remember that when spiritual writers refer in general terms to God's presence in and action upon their souls, they are and must be referring to that which the technical language of religion defines as the "work of the Holy Spirit." The abyss of the Godhead is unknown to us; and save under obviously inadequate symbols, cannot be thought of by us. Here the Thomist distinction between "sign" and "thing" is experienced by the soul in its extreme form. It is the Spirit indwelling and moving Creation that we really mean, when we speak of God experienced in prayer. Though the awe and rapture of the mystic, dazzled by glimpses of the Infinite, may find expression in the most transcendental language—still he remains a creature, subject to creaturely limitations; and his experience of Reality is of a creaturely kind. Thus Grou is surely speaking of God Immanent when he says: "The spiritual life is nothing but a commerce, an exchange, between God and the soul. God gives that He may receive, and receives that He may give. The soul does the same. He gives His prevenient grace to the soul in Time: He gives it unending glory in Eternity And this grace and this glory are a more or less perfect communication of God Himself." Here we see the mind at work bringing together the findings of direct experience and the findings of theological thought. Grou's language, harmonizing with that of many other mystical writers, indicates that "Grace" and "God" are not as a matter of fact to be distinguished in experience. Grace is the self-giving of the immanent Divine Life. It is a name for the generous, personal, manward-tending love and will of God. And prayer in its widest and deepest sense is the expression of the Godward-tending love and will of man. If we relieve both terms of their spatial suggestions—of all idea of transit, the coming from one place or plane and going to another place or plane—and think of this Holy Spirit, as St. Thomas says, as God wholly present "everywhere and at all times," we get a fresh vision of this double self-giving movement, this "commerce" of Spirit Uncreate and spirit created—which *is*, says Grou, the spiritual life —and of the worth and reality of prayer as depending on the degree in which it conforms to the condition of this exchange.

III

"Man," says St. Thomas again, "in so far as he is moved to act by the Spirit of God, becomes in a certain sense an instrument of God." And since in the life of prayer it is above all God who acts, and incites by His pressure man's activity, it follows that in all real prayer—whatever its apparent character—

the soul acts as the tool of the immanent Will and Love. This need not, of course, involve any consciousness of the Divine action: in fact, the greater the soul's simplicity and self-abandonment, the more that Divine action can and will overrule its small conscious activities. Every phase and type of prayer —Adoration, Communion, Impetration, Intercession —must be brought under this law. All apparent independence and spontaneity on the soul's part, all exercise of our limited freedom, all acts of will— genuinely ours, and most necessary to the soul's health, as seen from the side of the creature—yet depend for their very production on the prevenient and overruling action of God. It is a chief paradox of the spiritual life that its growth in power, its capacity for heroic and creative action, advance step by step with the realization of its own complete dependence on the supernatural:

> *Sine tuo numine*
> *Nihil est in homine,*
> *Nihil est innoxium.*

Yet this realization of dependence is saved from the limp passivity of the quietists by the fact that the Divine action is ever felt to deepen and energize the self's action; transform, absorb and use it, rather than abolish it. The exaggerated language of some contemplatives about "ceasing to act" seems due to their overwhelming sense of the Divine activity: but as a matter of fact we must regard their souls as energizing deeply in order to maintain this condition of fruitful abandonment to the energy of God. There is no such thing as the "holy idleness" with which they are sometimes charged. The two terms cancel each other: for sanctity, produced within the created order, can only be maintained by a constant tension, a willed surrender, a deliberate adherence of the will to God; which—though successive and perceptible acts may not be discerned in it—is none the less an action of the soul. This is what appears to be meant by the great saying of St. John of the Cross: "The whole wisdom of the saints consists in knowing how to direct the will vigorously towards God."

As we are nearer facts when we think of Spirit in terms of will than in terms of thought, so, too, prayer is on the whole best understood in terms of will and intention. True, in its advanced degrees, this will is chiefly manifest in a total movement of surrender, a mere placing of the soul in God's hand; and the further, deep action which results from this self-oblation is always felt to be the action of God rather than the deliberate action of the soul. Hence the external form taken by any one life of prayer matters little; except in so far as it avails to bring the praying soul into ever more complete harmony with the immanent Divine Will. And since the vocation of each soul within that great symphony differs, we need not be surprised by the wide diversities or even the apparent contradictions in *attrait* and in practice which are found in the world of prayer.

Seen from the human side, the energy of prayer seems to be exercised mainly in two directions—towards God, and towards men. We offer ourselves to God both as worshippers and as workmen, that our spiritual energy may be used to promote His purposes. It is true that many phrases of the great masters of prayer, taken alone and out of their context, would seem entirely to exclude that spiritual action of one soul on other souls for and in God, which is the essence of intercession, and would make the life of prayer consist entirely in adoration and adherence. But this contradiction is only apparent: and is simply a vigorous statement of the obligation to put first things first. The adoring surrender of the soul to God, and even a certain union with the immanent Holy Spirit, forms the one essential foundation of all intercessory action. For this depends primarily, not on the intensity of our sympathetic interest, our psychic sensitiveness or telepathic power—though all these may contribute to its effectiveness—but on a profound and selfless devotion to the purposes of the Divine Immanence. Even in the crudest, most naïve act of prayer, the soul lays itself open in some degree to that Divine action; and this movement, initiated by God, is completed and used by Him. Thus the purposive action of God and the soul collaborate in every prayer. "Feelings," "experiences," and all the rest, fade into insignificance before this most solemn privilege of men.

Adoration, then, is required of us as the condition of our entry into the supernatural action; as the temper of soul which alone maintains us within it, and gives to the praying self that suppleness and self-oblivion which make it amenable to the gentle impulsions of the immanent Spirit. Thus communion and collaboration, adherence and intercession, can never be separated in experience. They are the two aspects of that total life of prayer of which the key-word is to be *fiat voluntas tua*. Even while it moves, within the action of God, to an ever more complete individuation—a discovery and fulfilment of its unique task within the mystical body of praying souls—this life moves also to that profound surrender which places it, in action and in contemplation, wholly at the disposal of the living charity of God.

V

THE INSIDE OF LIFE[1]

D<small>R.</small> J<small>AMES</small> M<small>ARTINEAU</small>, the great Unitarian divine, used to tell a story of a young American, cultivated, intelligent and prosperous, who had come to Europe expressly to ask his advice. The American had no beliefs, except the belief that religion was a mischievous illusion; and for ten years he had steadily and publicly attacked religion with considerable success. But after a time he had somehow got uneasy. He had begun to feel that perhaps after all something was left out of his reading of life; that one could not be sure that all the side of existence which religion represents was mere delusion. And so he had given up his work and come to Europe; because he felt that he must find out whether there was something in religion after all. And now the question was: How was he going to find out?

Here was Dr. Martineau's prescription. He said: "You must give yourself a year; and you must spend that year in the same country, and with people of the same race. Live for the first six months among simple, slow-minded, narrow, even superstitious peasants, brought up in and practising a rigid traditional faith. Share their lives as intimately as you can. And then go for the second six months to alert, cultured, modern intellectuals, who have given up and despise all Church and all religion. And then

[1] Delivered as a broadcast address, December 13th, 1931, and published by A. R. Mowbray & Co. Ltd., by permission of the B.B.C.

ask yourself: which of these two groups of people—if either—has got that mysterious thing, a hold on the secret of life? Which knows best how to meet the deepest, most crucial realities of life—birth—suffering—joy—passion—sin—failure—loneliness—death?"

So the American went to Germany for a year, and then returned to report. He had spent six months in the home of a Westphalian peasant family; devout, narrow, ignorant, slow-minded and prejudiced people, full of superstitions, always treading on his toes, always offending his taste. "And what," said Dr. Martineau, "did they know of how to meet the deep realities of birth and death, love, suffering, sin?" The American said, "Everything." They seemed to have a sure touch, a wonderful conviction that went far beyond the crude way in which it was expressed. Their lives were entirely grasped and penetrated by something greater than themselves. And then he had spent six months in the student world of Berlin; among delightful, intelligent, keen-witted people, entirely emancipated from all moral and religious prejudices, with whom he had felt most sympathetic and thoroughly at home. "And what about these?" said Dr. Martineau. "How did they meet the dread and unescapable realities of life?" The American said, "They were helpless." No clue, no inwardness.[1]

Now I think that this story expresses with peculiar vividness the real cause of the so-called modern dilemma, in so far as it concerns religion. The cause, I believe, is the contrast, the opposition which modern life and modern culture tend to set up between breadth and depth; between the sharply focused

[1] This anecdote in its complete form appears in *Essays and Addresses*, by Baron von Hügel, Series ii, p. 126.

scientific truth which quickened the students' minds, and the dim, deep spiritual truth which nourished the peasants' souls. I suppose what the American had learned from his experience was this: that the life of those peasants, however rough and uncultured, had an invisible aim running through it which ennobled it. God and the soul mattered more to them than anything else. Their being was rooted in eternal realities. And this attitude of reverence towards the fundamental mysteries of our existence gave them in life's deepest moments an immense advantage over mere cleverness. The life of the Berlin intellectuals, so free, keen, alert and delightful, had no aim or significance beyond itself, no reverence. Confronted by the awful mysteries within which we move, they were without guidance or defence. They had no root in anything that endures. And those two groups of people, one rather dull and slow and faithful, the other very quick, critical, progressive; these exhibit, each in an exclusive way, the two great movements which are possible to the human spirit—one inwards, the other outwards. And both those movements are needed for a full, deep, and real human life. Because we are twofold creatures, we are not happy, we are not secure, we are not fully alive, until our life has an inside as well as an outside. We need the deeps of the world of spirit, as well as the wide and varied outer world of knowledge and of sense.

And here is where our modern dilemma comes in. Our generation has made such immense discoveries, has achieved such undreamed enrichments of the outside of life, that it has rather lost touch, I think, with the inside of life. It has forgotten the true riches and beauties of its spiritual inheritance: riches and beauties that go far beyond our modern chatter about values and ideals. The human mind's thirst for more and more breadth has obscured the human heart's craving for more and more depth. Not for the first time in human history, we are just now—at least many of us are—the dupes of our own cleverness. And because, in spite of this remarkable cleverness, it is very difficult for us to attend to more than a few things at a time, we leave out a great range of experience which comes in by another route and tells us of another kind of life. Our interest rushes out to the furthest limits of the universe, but we seldom take a sounding of the ocean beneath our restless keels. And then, like the American in the story, we get a queer feeling that we are leaving something out. Knowledge has grown. But wisdom, savouring the deep wonder and mystery of life: that lingers far behind. And so the life of the human spirit, which ought to maintain a delicate balance between the world visible and the world invisible, is thrown out of gear.

To put the whole matter in another and more homely way, the real modern dilemma is how we are going to reconcile the sort of truth declared in *The Mysterious Universe* with the sort of truth declared in "Hark! the herald angels sing." One series of truths belongs to life's outside—the other series belongs to life's inside. And to be a complete human being means to be in touch with both those worlds. The vast world of nature, stern and entrancing, where we are learning to spell out more and more of the poetry of God's creative thought: and the more vast, more stern, more entrancing world of spiritual experience, which alone gives meaning to that marvellous outer scene. It was Sir Thomas Browne who first called man the "great amphibium." We all

G

begin as tadpoles; but we ought to end as frogs—equally at home in both worlds, both elements. And the problem of how we are to do this, how we are to develop all our capacities and live eternal life within the world of time, takes a different form in each generation; though at bottom it is always the same problem.

The special form which it takes in our day seems to be this. Because the outer world and outer life are changing so much and so quickly, always showing us new possibilities, adding more and more new powers and experiences to our natural life, we feel that the inner world and its experiences have somehow become discredited and old-fashioned; that they have got to change too. We need a new heaven to match the new earth. But does that really follow? Six hundred years ago St. Francis, praying alone when he thought himself unobserved, found nothing to say but this: "My God and All! What art Thou? And what am I?" And in spite of the modern knowledge we are so proud of, the human soul is saying that still.

As a matter of fact, those remarkable changes that strike us so much when we observe the modern scene are mostly on life's surface. There are very few changes at life's heart. That is why great literature, however ancient, always moves us and is always understood. It has to do with the unchanging heart of life. And it is in the heart, not on the surface, that the world of religion makes itself known. "With Thee is the well of life, and in Thy light we see light." Does the theory of relativity really make any difference to that? I do not think so. We do not, after all, reconstruct our married life every time we move into a new and larger flat. The old, sacred intimacies remain. So too, the move-out of the human mind into a new and larger physical world, which is, I suppose, the great fact of our time, does not make any real difference to the soul's relation to God; even though it may make some difference to the language in which we describe Him. And the reason in both cases is surely the same.

The reason is that the deepest and most sacred relationships between human creatures—man and wife, parent and child, teacher and disciple, friend and friend—and the yet deeper relationship between the human creature and its Keeper and Creator, God: these are real facts, which go on and will go on, quite independently of what we think about them, or the degree in which we understand or feel them. If we treat these deep things with contempt, we merely cheapen our own lives. We do not make any difference to truth. If we leave them out, then we get a very incomplete picture of reality; the picture of a world which has an outside but no inside. But we do not alter reality. Clever as we are, we cannot manage that. Just as, if we choose to shut all our own windows, the room certainly gets stuffy; but we do not alter the quality of the fresh air outside. So the reality of God, the living atmosphere of Spirit, maintains its unalterable pressure; whether we acknowledge it or not.

One favourite, I might almost say popular, way of attacking the dilemma of faith has always been to seek in nature for some news, some evidence, about the Author of nature. That is of course a method with a very long history; and has always formed one of the strands in human religion. The writer of the eighth Psalm considered the heavens. Christ considered the lilies and the birds; and how characteristic that difference is, that coming down from the cosmic to the small and tender things—just as mysterious, just as holy as the nebula in Orion! "I can't," said Von Hügel, "really know even a daisy—why then should I expect to know the Being of God?" So Plato used the beauty of the earth to mount up to the other beauty. So St. Augustine says, "I understood Thy invisible things by means of the things that are made." And so now, we think we may perhaps find the invisible Truth in some new way "by means of the things that are made." Because the facts and measurements given to us by physical science disclose a wonderful measure and order in the world, we have been told that we may think of the Will behind the world as that of a great Mathematician. But if we think a bit about all those factors in life which suggest anything rather than mathematics—if we ask how a mathematical world is going to produce and to feed the lover, the poet, the saint—and then remember that some ultimate origin, some meaning must be found for them too, because they are real facts within the world; then we see that the guess about the Mathematician is no more adequate to man's experience of God and His creation, than the cook's guess that the Matterhorn must be a triumph of divine confectionery.

Turn now from all these attempts to explain the mysterious universe in the terms of our own little needs and notions and activities. Listen to the awe-struck and delighted language of the saints, who know the difference between the surface and the deeps of life, and know that it is always depth which matters most.

"Oh, Thou Supreme! most secret and most

present, most beautiful and strong! What shall I say, my God, my Life, my Holy Joy! What shall any man say when he speaks of Thee?"

That is St. Augustine. You are well beyond mathematics there, aren't you? Here is another—a woman this time:

"The eyes of my soul were opened, and I beheld the fullness of God. So that through excess of marvelling my soul cried out with a loud voice, saying: This whole world is full of God! and I understood how small a thing the whole world is— the abyss, the ocean, and all things, and how the power of God exceeds and fills all!"

"I abode," says another, "with a holy marvelling delight, joying in that which I saw."

There you see man standing at the spire-top of his spirit; forgetting himself and his own small affairs, gazing out on the unchanging immensities with awe and delight.

What about all that? Are we going to ignore this science of the saints, just as real and solid as any other kind of science, because it deals with invisible things? These men and women belong to a race that never dies out. In them we see the spirit of man gazing at reality; and not making guesses about reality, not trying to make it fit his own ideas, but swept by wonder and love. Wonder and love— those are great characters of the human spirit. All art is born of them and all religion too. It is wonder and love, more than any other two qualities, that make the difference between the human tadpole and the human frog. I am sure it is of the very essence of the modern dilemma to find a reading of reality which will give wonder and love—both together, not one alone—full value and full scope.

And it is here that organized religion, so distasteful in many ways to the modern mind, so often criticized and condemned, comes in—or ought to come in—to wake up and feed our poor dim sense of the beauty and aliveness of God. For the real business of the Church is not just what is sometimes called "surplice work." Its business is to bind us together—the learned and simple, the strong and the weak—in a great social act of love and worship: to provide a home for the nurturing of the spiritual life. For we cannot get on alone, in religion or anything else. Our spiritual life must be a social life too. We can each only manage a bit of it—it is far too big and various in its richness for any one soul. We must be content to pool our contributions, to learn from the past and learn from each other; humbly receive, and generously give. Wonder and love are caught, not taught: and to catch them we must be in an atmosphere where we are sure to find the germs. A living Church ought to be full of the germs of wonder and love.

I think that failure of the churches which we are always hearing about comes mainly from forgetting these facts. On one hand, we forget what the real function of a church is, and expect the wrong things from it. On the other hand, the Church, in its anxiety for custom, and to meet, as it says, the needs of the present day, has often tried to give us the wrong things. It has forgotten its true business— the production of holiness. Holiness; not just consolation, moral uplift or social reform. Its real job is to weave up men's love and wonder into worship; teach us that "holy marvelling delight in God." Its real stock-in-trade is the pearl of great price. It is not a general store. All its symbols and sacraments, all those services which ought to be great corporate works of art—all these are meant to train the souls of men to look up.

And surely modern men, gazing at the inconceivable vastness and splendour of the universe which science has disclosed to us, should be ready for this. That vision of the infinitely great and the infinitely small; and of the Mind of God, brooding over that universe, moulding it at every level and in every detail with the zest and inerrancy of love—this enlarging of our horizons and unselfing of our vision invites us, does it not, to worship and awe?

Adoration is the unchanging heart of religion, and the only key to its mysterious truths. There is no dilemma for the adoring soul. "Be still, and know!" "Those that wait upon the Lord shall renew their strength." The Church which teaches, nourishes and practises that adoring attention to God will never lose her hold on the hearts of men. That alone can make public worship the wonderful thing which it ought to be, and usually fails to be. But there is so much to do, there really is not time for all this, is there? Martha is busy with the cooking—she can't sit down and look. So many organizations, committees and practical questions of every sort and kind. And the poor Church is expected to attend to them all. Only lately, a London church advertised a sermon on the text, "Buy British": excellent practical advice, of course, but hardly the sort of sermon we should have heard on the Mount, driving its shaft into the hidden deeps of life, and disclosing the real nature of our link with God. And the business of religion is with that relation, and with those hidden deeps. Its aim is to give men eternity, and make them give themselves to eternity—that so, by this resort to the centre, they may integrate their whole existence, and learn how to make the practical surface of life significant and real. There is no other way of doing it. That is what those slow, uncultured, narrow peasants knew; and what the quick, charming, cultured, wide-minded students had missed.

Here, then, is the conclusion of the matter. We are called to live in two directions, not in one; and to obey two commandments, not one. We are not fully human until we do. For we are compound creatures, of sense and of spirit, of mind and of soul—dwellers in time, yet capable of eternity. Therefore nature alone is not going to content us; nor are the greatest triumphs of the intellect ever going to teach us the secret of life.

> Reason has moons, but moons not hers
>   Lie mirror'd on her sea,
> Confounding her astronomers,
>   But O! delighting me.

VI

WHAT IS MYSTICISM?[1]

WHAT is Mysticism? is a very difficult question to answer, unless we first deal with the things which mysticism is not, but with which it is too commonly confused. In spite of the great Christian mystical tradition which we have inherited, and because of the bad company the word often keeps, many people assume that it is merely another name for religious queerness or religious vagueness: for visions, voices, ecstasies and other symptoms of psychic instability, and even far less reputable forms of abnormality. Thus it has gradually become one of the most ambiguous and unsatisfactory words in the English language, arousing violent prejudice in those who hear it; and those who care most deeply for that which it really means often find themselves respecting the critics of mysticism far more than they respect many of its friends.

It is true that certain abnormal states of mind and even of body, which as yet we hardly understand, do sometimes appear in connection with mysticism, attracting an attention out of all proportion to their importance. But they can never be more than its by-products; and the tendency to exaggerate them has, more than any other cause, brought misunderstanding and discredit on the great souls of the mystics. A mystic is not a person who has queer experiences; but a person for whom God is the one reality of life, the supreme Object of love. He is a

[1] Published by A. R. Mowbray & Co. Ltd., 1936.

religious realist. Mysticism, then, far from being abnormal, is an essential part of all religion which is fully and deeply alive; it is the light which the mystics cast on the normal spiritual life, their disclosure of the landscape in which we really live, not their occasional excursions into an abnormal spiritual life, which gives them their great importance.

Francis Thompson, in that beautiful poem, "Any Saint," describes man as a

> Swinging-wicket, set
> Between
> The Unseen and Seen.

Man, that is, is the child both of the natural and the spiritual worlds. He is placed on the borderland; through him, there is a certain communication between them. In one way or another that is an idea which is quite familiar to us. We accept it, as we accept familiar food, without too much examination. But if we put that idea alongside one of our average acquaintances—or even alongside ourselves—we feel a certain contrast between the poet's view of humanity and our ordinary experience of humanity. We do not notice a general tendency in average men and women to swing out vigorously towards the Unseen, or even a marked desire to do so. The hinges of the wicket-gate seem to be differently adjusted in people of different types.

In many, it swings so widely and persistently open towards the visible side that nothing from the Unseen squeezes through. It is not noticed, and it is not missed. Those are the people who are commonly regarded as practical and sensible men. Their philosophy, unless it is a mere intellectual hobby unrelated to life, is always utilitarian. Their religion, when they have one, is practical, ethical, mainly expressed in fellowship and good works. They value it because it helps them to do their duty here and now; to live good lives. In some people, the wicket seems beautifully balanced. They take up and use together both sides of our wonderful human inheritance, moving to and fro between the temporal world and the eternal world, between communion with God and communion with their fellow-men; as Christ did during His life on earth. In a few, however, the hinges are so adjusted that, left to themselves, they always tend to swing out towards the Unseen. There they find, though they may not be able to describe it, the object of their love, and the whole meaning of their life. Those are the mystics.

So the beginning of an answer to the question, "What is mysticism?" must be this: Mysticism is the passionate longing of the soul for God, the Unseen Reality, loved, sought and adored in Himself for Himself alone. It is, to use a favourite phrase of Baron von Hügel, a "metaphysical thirst." A mystic is not a person who practises unusual forms of prayer, but a person whose life is ruled by this thirst. He feels and responds to the overwhelming attraction of God, is sensitive to that attraction; perhaps a little in the same way as the artist is sensitive to the mysterious attraction of visible beauty, and the musician to the mysterious attraction of harmonized sound. And as the painter comes to know a visible reality, a secret wonder revealed in form and colour, which wholly escapes the casual eye, and the musician to know a reality revealed in music of which the ordinary listener can only receive a fraction, and both are lifted by this experience to fresh levels of life; so the mystic, because of that loving and devoted attention which we call contemplation—"gazing into heaven with his ghostly eye," as one of them said—comes to know a spiritual reality to which we are deaf and blind. He knows it, but he cannot describe it; as we know but cannot describe the atmosphere of our own country, our own home. Its awful beauty and its living peace lie beyond the resources of our limited thought and clumsy tongues, which are adjusted to other levels of existence.

We begin, therefore, to see why mysticism has been called the science of the love of God; and why St. Augustine's great saying, "Thou hast made us for Thyself, and our hearts shall find no rest save in Thee," remains the best explanation of its undying appeal. For on the one hand, human beings do many hard and strange things when they are trying to express, or respond to, great love; and the real mystic always feels called to great sacrifices, much self-discipline, and the willing endurance of long periods of obscurity. The emphasis for him does not lie on his own wonderful experiences, his ardent and delightful feelings, his lovely visions, or anything like that. Very often his feelings are not ardent and delightful; and, even when they are, they carry with them a sense of obligation which kills all self-seeking, and compels him to consecrate the whole of his life to the purposes of God. He has seen Perfection, and wants to serve it, however much it costs. The life of the artist or musician, serving beauty and revealing beauty, is not easy. The life of the mystic, serving God, and by that very act revealing God, is harder still. For him, suffering and love are much the same thing—two forms of self-offering to God; and it is on God that the emphasis lies.

And, on the other hand, the knowledge that comes

through love is the only knowledge that is really worth having; and this is specially true of the knowledge of Reality, of God. "He may well be loved but not thought. . . . By love He may be gotten and holden, by thought never," said the greatest of our English mystics. This is not an invitation to religious emotionalism. It states a profound philosophical truth, which is a central truth of Christian theology too. The typical mystic, then, is the person who has a certain first-hand experience and knowledge of God through love; and the literature of mysticism tells us, or tries to tell us, what the finite human spirit has come to know through love of the relation between the little half-made spirit of man and the Infinite Spirit—God.

This experience of God may come in many ways and under many symbolic disguises. It may be steady or fleeting, dim or intense. But in so far as it is direct and intuitive it is always a mystical experience. Various things may result from it; a total change and reorientation of life, a long, hard discipline and inward growth, an immense transformation of personality, great creative power. Those whom we speak of as the great mystics are seldom dreamy contemplatives, but are people whose whole lives have been re-made in harmony with this overwhelming experience of God; and who have at last achieved that union with His spirit in which, as one of them said, they "are to the Eternal Goodness what his own hand is to a man," and act within the temporal order with a strange originality and power. St. Augustine and St. Francis, St. Catherine of Siena and St. Teresa, George Fox and Elizabeth Fry, are each in their different ways and degrees examples of this.

So a first-hand experience of God, the Absolute

Reality, and a life controlled by the overwhelming love which that experience awakens—this is what unites all mystics, Christian and non-Christian alike. As one of them said, they "mean only God, and none of His works," going straight beyond all symbols, definitions and images to the unspeakable fact of God, exceeding all that we can think or feel. They are the great experimental theists; so numerous and so distinctive that no theory of human knowledge, still less of human religion, which aims at completeness can possibly neglect their reports. The reports will vary, because the mystic, like the artist, is always showing us reality through his own temperament: a temperament which is immersed in history, and coloured by its social and religious surroundings. Only a few are able, like Ruysbroeck, to discriminate "between God and the light in which we see Him." But what matters to us and gives their great religious importance to the mystics is the massive agreement which underlies all their various experiences—the way these experiences, taken together, witness to the living fact of God and His relation to the created spirit of man.

St. Augustine's saying, "God is the only reality and we are only real in so far as we are in His order and He in us," gives us in a phrase the central conviction of every mystic; and we notice at once its intensely objective character. Their concern is with God. He is. That is what matters; not the ecstatic feelings which I may happen to have about him. For mystics, God is the fact of facts. They long for self-loss in Him, even while they know themselves eternally distinct from Him. For, intensely conscious of the contrast between His perfect and eternal Being and our imperfect changeful life, they know that only an effort and growth to ever closer union with that God, and at last a life so re-made in His order that He is all in all, can ever satisfy the soul's thirst.

So mysticism is man's conscious Godward trend; the response of his small dependent spirit to the pressure and invitation of the real God, the magnet of the universe. Such a definition as that relieves us from narrow and exclusive conceptions; since God's demand on the soul and call to the soul is a universal truth experienced by different men in many different ways and degrees. This definition, of course, begs the central question of theology—the very existence of God. But here we can hardly avoid that; for unless we accept the reality of God, mysticism ceases to have any meaning at all. When we speak of a mystic, we speak of a person who knows that his relation to this real God takes precedence of everything else; although this Godward longing and this Godward life may be expressed in many different ways.

I think this statement covers all the mystics; from the impersonal ecstasy of the pagan Plotinus with his longing to attain the One, to the Christocentric passion of St. Bernard or Richard Rolle and many others, who find in the Person of Christ the Divine Object of contemplation and love; from the Eucharistic mysticism of St. Thomas Aquinas or St. Catherine of Genoa, to the Inner Light of the Quaker saints. It shows us mysticism as the flaming heart of personal religion; and the mystic as a person whose function in the Church is to produce and keep burning this vivid sense of God. "Thou art great and dost wondrous things! Thou art God alone!" That is the substance of the mystic's affirmation. And over against that we have the deep longing of the soul for union with that transcendent God. "O knit my soul unto Thee!" says the Psalmist. That is the substance of the mystic's prayer. Where we find anyone whose life is ruled by this realistic passion for God, this inability to be satisfied with anything less than God, we are in the presence of a mystic; whether that life is lived inside or outside the cloister, inside or outside the Christian Church; and whatever the symbols he may use to describe or suggest the unseen Object of his love, whatever the work that love drives him to do.

This passion for God, this eager response of the soul to the living touch of God, appears within all the great religions. It must appear, I think, in any creed which has as its first term God, and which wakes human souls up to a realization of God; and as a matter of fact the Hindu, Moslem, and Jewish religions all have their mystics, their God-intoxicated men. When these speak of their desires and their experiences, they all, up to a point, seem to speak in the same tongue: for each is reaching out in its own way to the Eternal, and is speaking of that Object of love to which religion directs the soul of man.

"I should not exist, wert not Thou already with me!" says St. Augustine.

"I exist in God and am altogether His," says Rabi'a, the Mahommedan contemplative who has been called "the Moslem St. Teresa."

"My Me is God nor do I know my selfhood save in Him," says St. Catherine of Genoa, the lady of the Renaissance, who was the creator of modern hospital work.

"To be absorbed in God filled me with joy and delight," says the Franciscan Angela of Foligno.

"My hope is for union with Thee—that is the goal of my desire!" says Rabi'a again.

"Who dwelleth in love dwelleth in God," says St. John.

"From the beginning until the end of time there is love between me and Thee and how shall such love be extinguished?" says the Hindu Kabir.

"Thou art the love wherewith the heart loves Thee," says St. Augustine again.

"Thou dost fashion thy lovers to beauty and make them also worthy of love," says the pagan Plotinus.

There we have the typical declarations of the mystics; and it would be hard to pick out with a sure hand Christian from non-Christian in that list. There are ungenerous spirits who actually think that is a suspicious circumstance, and tends to discredit mysticism. But fortunately God is greater than their hearts, and the rewarder of all who diligently seek Him; whether or not they are on the Church roll.

All this surely means that the longing for God, the diligent search for Him, and the adoring delight in Him, are genuine characteristics of the human soul: and indeed that the human soul in which they seem to be absent has not yet developed its full powers. There is something in man which longs for the Perfect and the Unchanging, and is sure, in spite of the confusions, the evils, the rough and tumble of life, that the Perfect and the Unchanging is the Real. I believe this longing and this certainty are latent in everyone, in a more or less rudimentary condition, and that they are the best clue we possess to the mysterious nature of man and the true meaning of prayer. It is part of the business of organized worship to arouse and feed this Godward thirst, and so to make us more completely human, more alive. In many people it is dormant throughout life; in others, more or less awake even though dimly understood.

H

In a few the longing for Reality blazes up into a great passion, which triumphs over every obstacle and every other interest. The eternal Me, the indwelling spirit, emerges and recognizes that its home, its satisfaction, is not here. Its real home, its real satisfaction, is God.

If we leave these general ideas, and consider what mysticism is and means within Christianity we see that the great Christian mystical tradition, having its roots in the New Testament and including as it does some of the greatest of the saints, has a special quality which distinguishes it from those who have responded to the attraction of God from within other faiths. We should, of course, expect this, if the claim of Christianity to be a unique revelation of God, and the claim of the Church to be a supernatural society fostering the supernatural life of the soul, are true. Christianity is the religion of the Word Incarnate, and in the great Christian mystic something which has a certain relation to the mystery of the Incarnation takes place. He becomes at his full development a creative personality, a tool of God. The promise made in the first chapter of Acts is literally fulfilled in him; his loving contemplation of the Eternal, his prayer in the Spirit, produces power.

A non-Christian mystic, such as the great Plotinus, may describe his ecstatic experience of God as a solitary flight from this world with its demands, imperfections, and confusions, and a self-loss in the peace and blessedness of eternity. The Christian mystic knows these wonderful moments too; but for him they are only wonderful moments. His experience of eternal life includes the Incarnation, with its voluntary acceptance of all the circumstances of our common situation, its ministry of healing and enlightenment, its redemptive suffering. He cannot, therefore, contract out of existence with its tensions and demands. For him union with God means self-giving to the purposes of the divine energy and love.

Here is the secret of the strange power of St. Paul, St. Bernard, St. Francis, John Wesley, Elizabeth Fry, the Curé d'Ars, and thousands more. "Our works," says St. Teresa, speaking for all of them, "are the best proof that the favours we have received come from God." Thus she and her companion, St. John of the Cross, the prince of transcendentalists, labour and suffer for the reform of the religious life; Wesley takes the world for his parish; the Curé d'Ars becomes the conscience of France. "All Friends everywhere," said George Fox, "keep all your meetings waiting on the Light." That is a demand for a corporate act of mystical devotion; and we know what the lives of Friends in the world were required to be. All these endorse the saying of Ruysbroeck that the final state of the mystic is not ecstatic self-loss in the Godhead but something at once more difficult and more divine—"a widespreading love towards all in common." Indeed this must be so, because the God with whom he is united is the Absolute Love.

That which makes Christian mysticism so rich, deep, life-giving, and beautiful is, therefore, the Christian doctrine of the nature and action of God. It is different because it is based on the Incarnation, the redemptive self-giving of the Eternal Charity. The Christian mystic tries to continue in his own life Christ's balanced life of ceaseless communion with the Father and homely service to the crowd. His love of God and thirst for God have been cleansed by long discipline from all self-interest; and the more profound his contemplation of God, the more he loves the world and tries to serve it as a tool of the divine creative love. And indeed, a spiritual life which cuts the world into two mutually exclusive halves, and tries to achieve the Infinite by ignoring the finite and its obligations, could never be satisfactory for men; who need, in proportion to their spiritual enthusiasm, a constant remembrance of Plato's warning that it is not well to exercise the soul without the body or the body without the soul.

Though mysticism be indeed the living heart of all religion, this does not mean that religion does, or can, consist of nothing but heart. The Church is a Body with head, hands, feet, flesh, and hard bones: none of them any use, it is true, if the heart does not function, but all needed for the full expression of the Christian spiritual life. This acceptance of our whole life of thought, feeling, and action, as material to be transformed and used in our life towards God, is what Baron von Hügel meant by "inclusive mysticism." It alone is truly Christian; because its philosophic basis is the doctrine of the Incarnation, with its continuance in the Church and Sacraments. Its opposite, exclusive mysticism, the attempt to ascend to the vision of God by turning away from His creatures by an unmitigated other-worldliness, is not Christian at all. It ends, says that same great theologian, in something which cannot be distinguished from mere Pantheism: or, on more popular levels, in sloppy claims to be in tune with the Infinite.

Finally, the thoroughly organic, deeply human character of real mysticism is surely brought home to us when we see how gradually a mystic grows, what hard work he is called upon to do, and how many things he often has to suffer in getting rid of all that prevents him from swinging easily and peacefully between the Unseen and the Seen; how marked are the moral and psychological changes which must take place in him, and the different kinds of prayer which express his increasing communion with God.

Most people have heard of the "Mystic Way" with its three stages of Purgation, Illumination and Union. Though this ancient formula, borrowed by Christian writers from the Neo-Platonists, cannot be applied rigidly to all cases, it does in a general sense describe the great phases of growth which gradually make our ordinary, faulty, earthbound human nature capable of communion with the Eternal God. All indeed have to pass through a process much like this on their way to the full living-out of any kind of life. The artist, explorer, scientist, philanthropist, must root out everything that conflicts with his vocation and impedes his progress—all forms of self-occupation, pride, ambition, love of comfort; all competing interests, pleasures and affections—and such self-conquest is the very essence of the mystic's purgation. But the purity of heart demanded of him is much greater and more searching, because his objective is God, who asks his undivided devotedness and love. And because his special art, the medium of his communion with God, is prayer, this too must be developed, spiritualized, cleansed from self-will and self-interest and all unworthy images of God.

The reward of this courage and single-mindedness, this stern training in detachment, is always a great increase in knowledge and understanding. The power of the artist grows with his concentration; he is able to perceive and convey beauty in a way that he did not do before. So too the purified soul of the mystic, in proportion to his self-abandonment, sees all the truths of religion glowing with new beauty, reality and life. But the fullness and creative quality of the life to which he is called is only developed in him when he passes, and usually by way of great suffering, beyond this to a further stage: a state in which he is so penetrated, so sunk in and united to that divine life and divine beauty, that he seems to live in and with its very life, with the freedom, ease and simplicity of a fish at home in the sea. The mystics are fond of this metaphor—"I live in the ocean of God as a fish in the sea." That is the life of union, of conscious abiding in God; the full expansion of man's spiritual possibilities, and full satisfaction of his deepest desires. It brings with it great creative power. Once more we come back for our best definition to St. Paul's "I live, yet not I."

It is hardly strange that such a transformation of existence, such an ascent to the very summits of human nature, is seldom achieved; and costs those who do achieve it a good deal. We like to look on the spiritual life as something very noble, very holy; but also very peaceful and consoling. The word "contemplation" easily tempts those who have not tried it to think that the mystical life consists in looking at the Everlasting Hills, and having nice feelings about God. But the world of contemplation is really continuous with the world of prayer, in the same way as the high Alps are continuous with the lower pastures. To enter it means exchanging the lovely view for the austere reality: penetrating the strange hill-country, slogging up stony tracks in heavy boots, bearing fatigue and risking fog and storm, helping fellow-climbers at one's own cost. It means renouncing the hotel-life level of religion with its comforts and conveniences, and setting our face towards the snows; not for any personal ambition or enjoyment, but driven by the strange mountain love. "Thou hast made us for Thyself and our hearts shall have no rest save in Thee." Narrow rough paths, slippery shale, the glimpse of awful crevasses, terrible storms, cold, bewildering fog and darkness—all these wait for the genuine mountaineer. The great mystics experience all of them, and are well content so to do.

One of the best of all guides to these summits, St. John of the Cross, drew for his disciples a picturesque map of the route. It starts straight up a very narrow path. There are two much wider and better paths going left and right; one of them is marked "the advantages of this world" and the other "the advantages of the next world." Both must be avoided; for both end in the foot-hills, with no road further on. The real path goes very steeply up the mountain, to a place where St. John has written, "After this there is no path at all"; and the climber says with St. Paul, "Having nothing, I possess all things."

Here we are already a long way from the valley; and have reached the stage which is familiar to all climbers, when we feel exhilarated because we think we see the top, but are really about to begin the true climb. This is the Illuminative Life; and here, says St. John, on these levels, the majority of souls come to a halt. For the next thing he shows us is an immense precipice; towering above us, and separating the lovely Alpine pastures of the spiritual life from the awful silence of the Godhead, the mysterious region of the everlasting snows. No one can tell the climber how to tackle the precipice. Here he must be led by the Spirit of God; and his success must depend on his self-abandonment and his courage—his willingness to risk, to trust, and to endure to the very end. Every one suffers on the precipice. Here all landmarks and all guides seem to fail, and the naked soul must cling as best it can to the naked rock of reality. This is the experience which St. John calls in another place the Dark Night of the Spirit. It is a rare experience, but the only way to the real summit; the supernatural life of perfect union with the self-giving and outpouring love of God. There His reality, His honour and His glory alone remain; the very substance of the soul's perpetual joy. And that, and only that, is the mystic goal.

VII

I

The Priest's Life of Prayer

IT seems presumptuous for anyone, and especially a member of the laity, to attempt to add to that which has already been said and written upon the spiritual life of the Christian priest. Only the overwhelming importance of the subject for the work of the Church, and the fact that in the pressure of outward life we need again and again to be reminded of those unchanging realities of the inward life which alone give any value to our active work can justify this. But these certain truths are surely sufficient reason for considering once again the special nature of the priest's life of prayer; what it means, what it is for, and why it matters so much. It is true, of course, that in thinking of prayer we must guard against the inclination to regard it chiefly as a way of getting strength and help; a making use of God. Nevertheless, it is for the priest the unique source of pastoral power. Other things—intellectual and social aptitudes, good preaching, a capacity for organization—help his work, and help much. None of these, however, is essential. Prayer is. The man whose life is

[1] These two addresses were delivered to the Worcester Diocesan Clergy Convention at Oxford in September 1936, and afterwards printed in *Theology*. They were republished in response to requests from those who wished to possess them in a more permanent form by A. R. Mowbray & Co. Ltd.

121

coloured by prayer, whose loving communion with God comes first, will always win souls; because he shows them in his own life and person the attractiveness of reality, the demand, the transforming power of the spiritual life. His intellectual powers and the rest will not, comparatively speaking, matter much. The point is that he stands as a witness to that which he proclaims. The most persuasive preacher, the most devoted and untiring social worker, the most up-to-date theologian—unless loving devotion to God exceeds and enfolds these activities—will not win souls.

It follows from this, that the priest's life of prayer, his communion with God, is not only his primary obligation to the Church; it is also the only condition under which the work of the Christian ministry can be properly done. He is called, as the Book of Wisdom says, to be a "friend of God, and prophet": and will only be a good prophet in so far as he is really a friend of God. For his business is to lead men out towards eternity; and how can he do this unless it is a country in which he is at home? He is required to represent the peace of God in a troubled society; but that is impossible if he has not the habit of resorting to those deeps of the spirit where His Presence dwells.

We all know this; but it is desperately hard to keep our grasp of it, and go on putting it into practical effect. Everything in modern life, and perhaps especially in the life of the parish clergy, tends to make it more difficult. For the first thing that occurs to us is, that the mandate of Christ's minister is to feed and cherish His sheep, to give his life for that; and in most cases this is, and in all cases it can be, a full-time job. The demands on the time, interest, kindness, patience and energy of the faithful priest are constant, and must be met; for his model is One who serveth. So the determined setting aside, and holding against all comers as a first charge, of a substantial daily time for communion with God, might not in his case be justified if it were only done for the sake of his own soul. But it has a far greater sanction than that; and perhaps it will clear the real issue if we state this at once in the strongest terms. A priest's life of prayer is, in a peculiar sense, part of the great mystery of the Incarnation. He is meant to be one of the channels by and through which the Eternal God, manifested in time, acts within the human world; reaches out, seeks, touches and transforms human souls. His real position in the parish is that of a dedicated agent of the Divine Love. The Spirit of Christ, indwelling His Church, is to act through him.

It is true that God's freedom is absolute, and that He can and does act through all sorts of people, in all sorts of ways. But the priest has specially offered himself for this. Can anyone hope to fill such a position, unless his relation to God, his confident communion, and perpetual self-offering, is the first and most real thing in his life? He must be a living part of the Praying Church, take his full share in the life of the Praying Church, be woven into her eternal act of adoration, if his work among souls is to be done. He has to bring his people into the Presence of God, to offer in their name the sacrifice of praise and thanksgiving; and these are great and realistic spiritual actions, which demand in those who perform them a vivid spiritual life, and constant resort to spiritual food. If those who are set apart for this purpose do not put the supernatural first, no one else is likely to do so. And if in practice this is difficult, and means a tiresome wrench and readjustment of daily habits, God can never be adequately served or truly known except by the path of sacrifice.

Of course it is true that the direct worship of God does not cover the whole of the vocation of the clergy. The Christian minister is ordained to be both deacon and priest; the special character and grace of the diaconate is not obliterated when he receives the great privileges of the priesthood. He is still one of those called to serve the brethren, as well as to go up to the altar of God: and it is that double vocation, turned towards the Eternal and towards the human —love of God and love of souls—which makes the tension and richness of the priest's life, and must be reflected in his prayer. For him, at any rate, the disciplined and faithful cultivation of the inner life, the deepening of spiritual sensitiveness, can never be a self-regarding task: it is the very condition of his effectiveness.

All this means the maintenance of a right balance between the visible and invisible, active and contemplative sides of the religious vocation: adherence to God in prayer, and because of that adherence, supported and fed by it, a creative, cherishing, patient, redeeming love and service poured out to men.

When we come down from principles to practice, the demand on the strength and time of the parish priest is often so great that it seems as though this exclusive attention given to God is only to be had at the expense of time and attention which are needed by his people; that here, solitary communion with God is in the nature of a spiritual self-indulgence, and that detailed response to the demands and needs of the flock must always be nearer to the mind of

Christ. But surely Christian history steadily contradicts that view. It is always the priest whose life of prayer is deep and strong, and a first charge on his time, whose work for God and souls is also deep and strong; who is ready for the self-forgetful labour and constant sacrifice which it requires. The vocation of the Christian minister is a supernatural vocation; and how can he fulfil it unless he lives a supernatural life? Much is now being said about evangelism; but before we get effective evangelism, we have to get effective evangelists. Evangelism is useless unless it is the work of one devoted to God, willing and glad to suffer all things for God, penetrated by the attractiveness of God. New machinery, adaptations and adjustments, are not the first need of the Church of England; but more devoted, adoring, sacrificial souls. These are supernatural qualities, given by God in our hours of direct attention to Him; and these are the only lasting source of that charity, that invincible loving-kindness which will help us to show the beauty of Christ to others and so win them for God. It is terribly hard for human beings to believe this, believe it enough to carry it out; but those who do carry it out have no doubt of its truth.

Consider the Curé d'Ars, the pattern and patron saint of parish priests. There was a man of very humble origins, of very limited intellectual power, and with the minimum of education needed for his career; but with the maximum of devotedness. From the human point of view, this was his total equipment. At a very difficult moment in the history of the French Church, he was sent to a particularly hopeless village, where religion and morals had gone to seed; and there he spent his whole life. No preferment, no external help either spiritual or material, no apparent scope. Yet bit by bit, as his spiritual power developed, and the strange magnetism of a living Christianity was felt, this poor, obscure peasant priest became the conscience of France, the determining influence in thousands of lives. His church was a place of pilgrimage for a multitude of troubled souls from every part of the country. There was no reason for this except the power of God, acting through a loving and abandoned soul transformed by prayer. Not many clergy would care to tackle his average working day. The number of hours which he spent in pastoral work, or in his church—either in worship, or in ministering to those who came to him—often amounted to sixteen out of the twenty-four. So long as anyone needed him, he just went on and on. But this intimidating programme, and this untiring love and care for souls, still left time for that which made it possible: the deep personal life of prayer, self-offering, communion, supplication—loving, realistic, confident intercourse with God.

Again, come to an example from our own times and our own Church: the career of Father Wainright of St. Peter's, London Docks. Fifty years in one parish; which was hardly civilized when he came to it, but "washed by the tears of his people," as one of them said, when he died. Fifty years spent not in ministering to the respectable members of the congregation, but in constant devotion to the lost sheep, the drunkard, the degraded and the criminal; appearing in the middle of the night unasked at the bedside of the dying, and bringing security and peace. We can realize something of the spiritual and the physical demands of such a career as that; the staying power it requires. How was it done? It was done in the strength drawn from a constant communion with

God; supported and expressed by the daily Eucharist, and by the hour of absorbed devotion which followed it and which no call was allowed to interrupt. I suppose there are few Christians who would not be thankful to accomplish a tithe of what Father Wainright did for Dockland; but the way in which he did it is the only way in which such work can be done. First the inward and secret life of oblation and adherence to God; and then in its power, the outward life of co-operation with God. To do great things for souls, you must become the agent and channel of a more than human love; and this must be the chief object of a priest's life of prayer. It means a most careful preservation of our Lord's balance between solitary communion with the Father and loving self-spending among men.

We turn from this to strictly practical considerations. Accepting this fact that the Godward life, the prayer of the priest is his first duty, indeed his first necessity: what are the lines on which it can best be developed? His time is limited by his various obligations; even though the first charge on that time be his secret communion with God. Moreover, he shares with all other human beings the humiliating fact that our attention to things of the Spirit cannot be suddenly produced, or sustained beyond a certain point. Even at best it will fluctuate a great deal; and often needs preparation and support. So he is not only limited from outside by his pastoral duties, but also from within by the very facts of our human nature. Therefore his devotional life must be planned with prudence as well as with fervour. Even that quiet, speechless waiting on God, that trustful self-abandonment to His purposes, which is one of the most deeply refreshing of all prayers, is always apt to fall away into wandering thoughts or mere drowsiness if we presume, and try to maintain it too long; or do not feed it wisely by thoughts and by reading which tend to deepen in us the sense of God's greatness and the spirit of adoring love. Therefore it is well to let the reading and vocal prayer which feed and prepare the times of mental prayer be always about God, and not about men. We should dwell most on the mighty, positive qualities of the Eternal; "mean God, not His works," as the mystics say. "He alone matters, He alone *is*." The priest, so beset by the problems and needs of men, should frequent in his reading the society of those who know this, and try to catch something of their spaciousness of mind, their deep realism, their devoted love: should let God flood his life, and then, in His light and power, confront the problems of that life.

Again, there are days for everyone when the forms of our prayer become dead, tasteless and unreal to us; sometimes indeed almost repugnant. The Offices are dreary and meaningless; and we can produce nothing of our own. Our ceiling, as airmen say, is low. No one escapes this experience; and the character of his life, his constant preoccupation with religion, must keep the priest specially exposed to it, and make it specially painful in his case. For whatever he may feel, or not feel, he must still try to present religion in its freshness and attraction—even though it seems stale, unattractive, unreal—deliberately discounting his own misfortunes and practising the most searching self-oblivion at the very heart of his spiritual life.

All this means that the prayer of the priest must never be allowed to become too individualistic and subjective. He needs the constant support which is given by remembrance of his corporate situation, as a member of the one supra-personal Praying Church; the constant sense that the prayer of that great Church goes on, and we, whatever our feelings or our failings, are an integral part of her life. *She* offers the one sacrifice of praise and thanksgiving. We sink our small lives and small spiritual efforts in that great worshipping life; carrying on, as faithful members of that Body, through the periods of spiritual darkness as well as the periods of spiritual light.

Ye that by night stand in the house of the Lord: even in the courts of the house of our God,
Lift up your hands in the sanctuary: and praise the Lord.

There is always a night-shift, and sooner or later we shall find ourselves serving on the night-shift; and if our prayer is mainly of the individual and subjective sort, giving too much space to feeling and not enough place to will, it puts us in a very poor position. What we all need then, and the priest I suppose needs very specially, is some link between our own fluctuating communion with God and the great continuous action of the Church; a devotional pattern, a reminder of the vast life of prayer coming out of the past, stretching forward to the future, into which our small prayer is woven; something which shall steady us, transcend our changing feelings, and keep our minds in tune with the Mind of the Church.

The priest, of course, has this pattern laid down for him; a pattern in which all the deepest spiritual truths of Christianity are gathered up and conserved. The great outlines of his life of prayer are already drawn in the Divine Office, which he must recite morning and evening in union with the whole

I

Church, and in the Eucharist, which it is his sacred privilege to celebrate. And in a general sense we may say that it is by deepening and enlarging the dispositions which these great acts of worship demand and foster that his spiritual life will grow best. If he pours into this mould all that he can of his adoration, his penitence, his self-naughting and his love, and so makes it—as he can do—the living instrument of his converse with God, he needs nothing more. He is then part of the great life of the Praying Church; and his personal life of prayer, which so easily becomes lonely, thin and worried, at the mercy of passing moods if cut off from that of the main body, gains dignity and power, for it is offered in and with Christ, by whose Spirit the Church lives.

Look first then at the daily Office, as the material, the ordained vehicle of the priest's daily prayer. What is it? Essentially, it is a beautifully balanced act of pure worship. "Praise ye the Lord! The Lord's Name be praised!" Its material is nearly all Biblical; so that here Evangelical and Catholic are at one. By far the larger part—the psalms and the canticles—is great Christian poetry, charged with inexhaustible meaning; suggesting far more than it says, and capable of lifting up those who use it rightly, and introducing them into the atmosphere of eternity.

Surely it is a very great thing that twice every day the Christian minister must withdraw his attention from all the details and demands which beset him, feed his prayer by reading and meditation of the Scriptures, and yield to the influence of this sacred poetry—the *Venite, Te Deum, Magnificat*—with its dominant mood of adoring and disinterested delight. What a tragedy that this part of a priest's duty, which can lead him out to the supernatural, and is inexhaustible in its spiritual suggestions, should ever become formal, hurried, unreal! See how the Western Church, from the earliest times, has put the *Venite* at the beginning of the great Office of Matins which opens her daily cycle of prayer; to give straight away the colour and accent of her worship. All her ministers are required to adore God under this formula every day; to come before His presence with thanksgiving, and show themselves glad in Him with psalms. That is the temper in which the Offices should be said. "Leave the transitory, seek the Eternal," says Thomas à Kempis. Twice a day the Divine Office calls us, for our soul's health, to do this. Not the *Miserere* but the *Venite*; not subjective penitence, but objective delight in God. "O Lord, open *Thou* my lips; and my mouth shall show forth Thy praise." We begin with the direct appeal to God as the only cause and author of prayer; take a Bible into our hands, and look confidently up to Him.

The Church of England, in selecting from the Breviary the material for her Morning and Evening Office, seems specially to have desired to emphasize this note of worshipping joy. Every morning, as well as the *Venite* and *Benedictus*, the *Te Deum* or the *Benedicite* is to be said or sung. Those glorious songs, if we mean them, ought to be enough to send Christians off for the day's work in very good spirits; more focused on God's splendour than on their own difficulties. We all know well enough how hard this temper is to maintain through the tensions and ups and downs of life—anxiety, pressure, disappointment, loneliness, ill health—but how magnificent it is that every day the Church decisively calls her sacred ministers to return to this note of triumph and joy;

to contemplate the loveliness of God. "He whom God pleases, pleases God," said St. Augustine. There we have in a nutshell the meaning of adoring prayer. And only the priest whom God really pleases is going to make others really care about God.

So adoration is to stand first in the priest's ordered prayer; and all he says and does is to be coloured by this. In fact, the rhythm and proportion of the Lord's Prayer should be the rhythm and proportion of his whole life of prayer; first God in Himself and his worship of God and relation to God—our Father who art in heaven, hallowed be Thy Name—then, and only then, our human situation and needs. God in His Holy Perfection, the Father of all Life, already completely present, bathing and penetrating us. "O come, let us sing unto the Lord!" The prevenience of God and adoration of God are the dominant facts of the life of prayer, and especially of the priest's life of prayer; for such adoration means getting our attitude to Reality right, and keeping it right. It is the essential preparation of all decent action; and especially of all religious and pastoral action. The Christian priest is called to be a fellow-worker with God and a yoke-fellow with Christ, both pulling at the same cart; and the object of his life of prayer is to keep him fit for this glorious privilege, weld him ever more and more into the organism—the Church—that is working for the triumph of God. It is to set the scene for his penitence, his moral striving and his devotedness—for that deep and intimate conversation, as of one friend with another, which is the cause and support of the consecrated life; and in which we at last learn to say, without any reserves and without counting the cost, "Thy Will be done."

"God," says Paul Claudel, "keeps up a continual

conversation with every creature." He has a special conversation to maintain with each one of us; and the traditional praise and prayer of the Church, rightly practised, is a wonderful means of tuning us in to it. When the conversation is established, and in the words of Pusey's beautiful prayer we have "escaped from the weary round of harassing thoughts into His Eternal Presence," then and only then can we rightly offer our petitions; as in the Divine Office these follow the psalms, canticles, and lessons, that is to say, the adoring and meditative parts of our prayer. Sometimes, it is true, the conversation will be mainly a confession of faults or a disclosure of weakness or depression; but this, too, can be brought into the tranquil presence of God and have its quality changed by contact with His reality. It is this sequence of praise, attention and prayer which gradually trains us to a complete suppleness in His hand, a total acquiescence in His mysterious purpose; so that our actions become, more and more, the actions of the Holy Spirit in us. This alone is to be in a true sense a minister of the Gospel; that is, an agent of God's self-expression in the world. Unless the priest's will is thus turned to God—unless God is his magnet, his true centre of interest—his prayers of supplication, for light and strength in his work, for his people and their needs, for sinners, will not be truly alive or truly real.

The daily Offices, then, can and should provide a frame for the priest's daily prayer, with its varied movements of adoration, penitence, meditation on the Word of God, and supplication to God. But all this has reality and worth because of something far deeper—something which involves the very life of the soul—and this deeper life and movement is embodied and expressed in the liturgy of the Eucharist, the great central act of Christian worship.

The rhythm and movement of the Eucharist show forth in a wonderful way the true rhythm and movement of the ministerial life; which is, of course, a part of the great rhythm and movement of the Church's life. That is to say, it is first an offering made to God, an oblation; and a consecration to His purpose of that which is offered—our life. And next, it is a return movement to men, bringing to them the Food of Eternal Life; and a fellowship in the receiving of that gift. For the Eucharistic mystery is the outward and visible expression of that Eucharistic life by and for which the Church exists; a natural life given in its wholeness to God, laid on His altar, like its tokens, the natural elements of bread and wine, and consecrated, transformed by His inpouring life, to be used by Him to give life and food to other souls. And this is surely the essence of the priest's vocation. "You are the Body of Christ," said St. Augustine to his communicants. You are meant to be offered as a reasonable and living sacrifice; and so made the vehicles of His self-imparting love. With what great and searching force that saying comes to the priest. Whenever the Church celebrates the Eucharist, she performs her supreme act of worship; and she also celebrates the mystery of her being. A minister of religion is not only a bit of that living Church, but a member specially set apart for this sacred work. That fact, that tremendous vocation, must surely dominate his life of prayer; which must be penetrated by the twin dispositions of total self-offering to God, and of total dependence on God. Here every priest is allowed to share the central religious experience of the saints; comes up to the frontiers of the supernatural, stands in that Upper Room whose window opens towards Calvary, commemorates in awe and joy the great movement of charity of which the Church was born, and renews the sacred action in and through which the divine self-giving is set forth, the soul is nourished, and the Church and her Master meet. His own private prayer can hardly fail to be deeply coloured by this great religious act; or, as it grows in depth and breadth, to be more and more harmonized to the rhythm of the Eucharistic life, as various branches of the Catholic Church set it before us.

There is no need to dwell on the first part of the service, the prayers of approach and the Ministry of the Word. All this, of course, has its obvious counterpart in the reading, meditation, and prayer, the faithful discipline of mind and heart, which prepare, support and condition our life of communion with God. But far more important for the priest's own interior life are the implications of that great movement of self-giving and approach to God which begins with the Offertory, and rises to its culmination in the Eucharistic prayer.

The Offertory is now so reduced and identified with the collection that we almost forget its great liturgical and spiritual significance. Yet it still represents the actual oblation of the bread and wine, the raw material of communion, which God is to accept and consecrate, and so by implication the offering to Him for His purpose of the whole of our natural life, the cost, the sacrifice without which there is no living prayer; and beyond that the self-offering of the whole Church in and with Christ her Head, for the giving of more abundant life to the world. So here we have given at once the essential disposition of the celebrant's soul. For the oblation to God which must be made by him is so searching and so complete, so much the heart of his vocation, that this ever-renewed act of self-offering must always stand in the foreground of his prayer. "Take, Lord, and receive all my liberty—all I have and possess!" everything for him is and must be conditioned by this. His deepest religious preferences and longings, no less than his human desires, must take second place over against God's demands and his flock's needs. He is often required to give them the food of Eternal Life in what may seem to him a very crude and unappetizing form; and unite with them in the approach to God which they understand, but from which his temperament and taste recoil. This and much else will enter into that self-offering which Thomas à Kempis thought the one essential preparation for the celebration of the Eucharist: "Whatsoever thou givest beside thyself, I regard it not; for I look not for thy gifts but for thee."

It is after this oblation, and because of it, that the Church comes to the second great phase of her prayer; when she turns back to the needs of the world and offers the "great intercession," represented in our rite by the prayer for the Church Militant, for all conditions of men. For self-oblation—sacrifice—is the only adequate preparation for the prayer of intercession which prevails with God. It means that our solemn self-offering under tokens is accepted and used by Him. This, too, must be reflected in the movement of the priest's life of prayer. "I will offer the sacrifice of thanksgiving, and will call upon the Name of the Lord." He must bring all for whom he prays with him in his approach to God; and offer himself, his whole life, for them. This devoted supplication for his people, held up to God with cherishing love, is probably the most effective spiritual instrument of his ministerial work. Because we are all "one loaf," the sacrificial prayer of even one humble soul does something for all. It is a supernatural action, a necessary part of the Eucharistic life. Intercessory prayer for others completes self-giving prayer to God. It is the stretching out of the arms on the Cross of life, to embrace the world's need; redemptive action. With these two movements established at the heart of his devotion, the Christian priest is a tool in the hand of God; possessed by His charity, a channel through which He can work. We are very far yet from realizing what a priest can do for his people in the world of sacrificial, intercessory prayer; bringing all the vicissitudes of life, all their sins, failures, hopes, needs, griefs into relation with the Divine Love.

What comes next? The movement towards heavenly places, in the Preface and the *Sanctus*: adoration, the vision of Holiness, the recognition of the glory, the Otherness of God. Christianity is a religion of contrasts; and Christian prayer too, especially in its priestly aspect, is to embrace the extremes of joy and penitence, the splendour and holiness of God, the littleness and neediness of man. "Glory be to Thee! Have mercy on me!" The right prelude to the mystery of consecration and to the remembrance of Christ's Passion is the vision of the Divine Beauty, and a grateful and awestruck thanksgiving for that beauty; uniting ourselves with the humble yet exultant song of the Seraphim, reminding us of the greatness of that spiritual world enfolding and penetrating us, within which our sacrifice of praise and thanksgiving is made.

Consecration does not, of course, mean something

that we do. It is something that God does. Here, in our secret prayer as well as our liturgic prayer, our action ceases, and His action begins. We have offered something. He transforms it; lifts it to a new level of reality which it could never achieve on its own, makes it a vehicle of His own self-given life. A consecrated life, therefore, which must be the goal of the priest's interior prayer, is a life which, having been offered without reserve, is transformed by God and made what it ought to be; a sacrament of His life and love, a means whereby that life and that love are communicated to other souls. It is as sharing in some faint degree in our Lord's High-Priestly action, bringing the needs of the world to the altar of God, and going forth from the altar of God bringing bread and wine to the needs of the world, that the Christian priest's life of prayer must be lived. And this rich life of prayer, again and again bringing him close to things infinite and eternal, yet never separating him from the natural life, he shall lift up to God, offer in its wholeness, for the manifold needs of men. Here is the mould into which he can pour all his thirst for God, all his self-giving to God, all his love and concern for souls.

II

The Life of Prayer in the Parish

We go on to consider how the parish priest can best draw his people, in the various ways and degrees suited to them, into the life of prayer; wake up their sense of God, and develop their latent spiritual capacities. That, of course, is his central task as a shepherd of souls. He is called to the building up of Christian personalities; and there is no Christian personality where the life is not based on virtual or actual prayer. I am not one of those people who think that prayer can be taught, or that the many excellent text-books on the subject can by themselves cause one single soul to pray. God and God alone can reveal to the soul its capacity for communion with Him; and until He does so, whatever other people may tell it about prayer, it remains ignorant of what prayer really is. But it is possible to prepare the ground; to convey by suggestion that which cannot be conveyed in set terms, clear away obstacles, create a favourable atmosphere for the emergence of the spirit of prayer.

What, then, are the chief factors which the parish priest has at his disposal for this purpose? Primarily, I think, they are three. First, his own life of prayer, his communion with God; next, the parish church, and that which is done in it; last, the formation of praying groups. We begin therefore by considering the matter under these three heads.

First, the priest's own devotional life. This is decisive. The primary way in which he can lead his people to pray is by doing it himself . The spirit of prayer is far more easily caught than taught. By a very large proportion of his flock, its nature will only be realized in so far as they see it in him, and discover that for him it is the very substance of life. "For their sakes I sanctify Myself." That text has a most searching application to the priestly members of the Body of Christ. Cold, perfunctory, negligent prayer in the minister of religion is not only a personal fault and personal loss. It is a sin against his people; he fails his neighbour in a vital matter, as well as failing

God. Therefore the first step towards deepening the life of prayer in a parish, is nearly always deepening it in the life of the parish priest. It has to begin somewhere; and we cannot count on its beginning anywhere else.

In the letters of that great teacher of souls, the Abbé de Tourville, there is a passage in which he describes how he found himself confronted by the problem of teaching others how to live the life of prayer, under conditions of great personal difficulty as to health and other limitations: and how he realized that the essential point was that he himself must be, and go on being, his own first pupil. All those qualities of humble dependence on God, love, faithfulness, courage, self-oblivion and tranquillity of soul which it demands could only be imparted in so far as he possessed and fostered them in himself. I am sure that this is the root of the matter. The old-fashioned phrase about "leading" others in prayer has a deep truth in it. The shepherd goes before, and the sheep follow after; some of them at any rate. Therefore the shepherd of souls does best, not when he turns to his people to teach and exhort them—though of course that has its place—but when he turns towards God and goes before them. It is always by that which he does, not by that which he says, that they will learn the secret of prayer.

The priest who prays often in his own church, for whom it is a spiritual home, a place where he meets God, is the only one who has any chance of persuading his people to pray in *their* own church. True devotion can only be taught by the direct method. The mere presence and atmosphere of a pastor who does what he says, and does more than he says—for whom prayer is the central reality of life—who comes early into his church to make his preparation before the Eucharist, is absorbed in that which he is going to do, does it with recollection and love, and returns to the church to make his thanksgiving among those to whom he has given the Bread of Life—this teaches prayer. So, too, the saying of Matins and Evensong in church is a most valuable help to the same end. Even though the priest may often do this alone, the very fact that he does it counts. It is an act of devotion to God, done for his people; and if it entails a sacrifice of convenience or time, all the better.

It is noticeable that those who do not set much store by institutional religion, always respect those whose religious practices cost them something, and who fulfil the religious obligations which they have taken on. Many who cannot or will not join in liturgical worship will yet be made to take that worship more seriously than before, because the parish priest is seen to find time for it, and shows it to be for him one of the ruling realities of daily life. Izaak Walton, in his life of George Herbert, describes how Mr. Herbert went twice every day to his church of Bemerton, rang the bell and said his daily Office; and because all the common people loved him dearly, how even the ploughman would pause in his ploughing when "Mr. Herbert's saints' bell rang to prayers." That might still happen; and if it did, it would mean that twice a day the spirit of prayer was radiating from the church, which is intended as its visible shrine and abiding place, to permeate the common life of the parish.

To achieve this, if he can do so, is surely a part of the vocation of every parish priest. It is true that only a minority of the parishioners will be affected; and at first perhaps no one will be affected. Here as elsewhere the minister of Christ must be prepared to endure much spiritual loneliness, and dispense with outward signs of success. But this fact must never discourage us. All the effective things in the history of the Church have been begun by individuals, and done by small groups. "The Holy Spirit," said Bishop Gore, "always works through minorities." In every parish, it is certain that the spiritually alert, those who are already disposed to prayer, will be in the minority. But it is of the first importance for the priest to get hold of them, ally himself with them, instruct and encourage them; make a nucleus and start there. That was our Lord's method; the little group of devoted souls as the instruments of wider evangelization.

Of course the fact that he conducts the services gives the priest an unparalleled opportunity to train his congregation in prayer. In those services, every aspect of the life of prayer is expressed; penitence and trust, adoration and thanksgiving, self-offering and confident demand, devotion to Christ and praise of the Eternal God. In so far as he gives these great spiritual actions their full reality and worth, he is teaching by demonstration what worship is. The services of the Church are the real schools of prayer, when they are used rightly; and when the congregation is helped, far more than is usually done, to understand the full significance of the various parts of Morning and Evening Prayer and the Eucharist.

After the careful and disciplined development of his personal life towards God, I think the priest's next step in teaching his people to pray, in so far as this is possible, will be the bit-by-bit interpretation of the services. A complete transformation of their attitude to those services can be effected by showing them what the liturgy means and is, what tremendous realities it expresses; getting behind the beautiful Tudor English, and the symbolism which so often means nothing to those who use it, and revealing the great spiritual action in which we take part when we join the Church's corporate worship. And further, linking this spiritual action—of which the liturgy is the outward dress—with the actualities of daily life on one hand, and the unchanging fact of God on the other hand.

Of course there are plenty of useful little books on these subjects in the tract-case; but only a minority are going to buy and study the contents of the tract-case, and generally those who least need to do so— the people who are already interested in the details of worship. Nor will reading have the same effect as oral teaching about the meaning of the services, given in the church where they worship, by the clergyman with whom they worship. There are many parishes where "Down with the Sermon, and up with the Instruction" would alone work a great renewal of devotional life. The mere information, for instance, that the collect of the day is meant to collect and present before God all the secret prayers of the faithful, and should be accompanied by a silent act of prayer, is news to a surprising number of instructed Christians. So too plain addresses, with knowledge behind them, about what the psalms and canticles mean, and with what intention they are used by the Church, what spiritual riches are hidden in them, and what great dispositions and needs of the soul they imply—translating and interpreting the service bit by bit—this will be rewarded by the creation of an interested, intelligent and really corporate parochial worship.

I hesitate to appeal to personal experience as regards the extent to which this is needed; but I will say this. A short time ago I gave a series of retreat addresses on the Lord's Prayer. They did not deal in high or peculiar spiritual doctrine; but did try to bring out the real meaning and balance of the prayer —which is, of course, a complete direction for the life of communion with God. The result of these simple instructions was startling. Person after person—all educated churchwomen, sufficiently drawn to the life of prayer to come into retreat—came to me saying that they had never before realized the meaning and scope of the prayer; and several frankly confessed that they had always found it boring. A set of addresses on the Holy Communion Service had very much the same result. I became convinced that here there is great scope for teaching; and that only a minority of practising Anglicans now make the connection between the formulas of the Prayer Book and the deep realities of the life of prayer, which those formulas are intended to express, and indeed do express. This means that they have only a very vague idea of what it is that they are doing when they take part in the Church's liturgical life; and if they only have that, they will not be deeply interested in doing it.

We go on to the priest's second asset: the parish church, considered not as a convenient place for Sunday worship, but as a House of Prayer, a home of the Spirit, a place set apart for the exclusive purpose of communion with God; and therefore an abiding witness to His reality, His attraction, His demand. In that building and all that it stands for, he has his great opportunity for making prayer a vivid fact in parochial life. It goes without saying that the church will be kept open. The open church is already a visible symbol of the loving welcome atmosphere; and possibly its priest and those who think with him will have to pray in it much, before that atmosphere is produced. Nevertheless, it can be produced. Nothing is more marked, to people of even a moderate degree of sensitiveness, than the difference between the bleak frowstiness of the "convenient place of worship" left empty all the week, and the home-like air of the church which its people—even a few people—frequent for prayer. It is useless to put the usual little notice in the porch about prayer and meditation unless a real effort is made to turn the church into a place where people desire to pray, and can pray. Such things, of course, as the homely and attractive Children's Corner, or the chapel which is used for weekday services, and is kept fresh with flowers and furnished with devotional books, come in to help. But that which helps most is the friendly shelter of a building which is wholly dedicated to intercourse with the Unseen, and therefore full of suggestions which help our attention to God; the separation it effects from the sounds, demands, and complications of everyday life, the quiet and security from interruption. The church is there to give all this; and in giving it, to provide a powerful stimulus to prayer.

Of course people, and especially English people, need a great deal of support and encouragement if they are to form the habit of using their church for prayer; but all the efforts made in this direction, in sermons, teaching, private conversation, and example, are more than worth while. Young people, especially confirmation candidates and guild members, should be trained to regard this as the normal

K

thing to do. Many of them have no other chance of privacy; and it is useless to insist on the importance of prayer, or to speak to their elders on the strength and tranquillity which come from the habit of silent waiting on God, unless some attempt is made to provide them with suitable conditions. There are already many churches, in London and large towns, which are such homes of prayer; where people come in and out during the whole day, and especially after work in the evening, to dwell for a little while on the things of God and "escape from the weary round of harassing thoughts into His Eternal Presence." There might be, and ought to be, such a living church in every parish, accepted as a matter of course and used as a matter of course; if its immense spiritual importance were realized, and those responsible for the religious life of the parish were determined at all costs to bring it into existence, whatever the apparent difficulties might be.

This brings us to the last of the three resources which every parish priest has at his disposal, for the fostering of the life of prayer among his people; the formation of the praying group. I do not mean by this a hot-housy association of pious ladies, whose extreme exhibition of fervour too often tends to put everyone else off. This should be avoided at all costs. But there is surely no parish where it is quite impossible to find a few people, preferably quite simple and ordinary people, who care for their religion, and, if asked to do a bit of real spiritual work for it, will respond. These are the people who can form, as it were, the growing-point of the parochial life of prayer. They will probably be found among the more frequent communicants; among those who are already doing some kind of parish work; and very often,

among the quiet, diffident, rather unnoticed members
of the congregation. They should be asked personally
and individually—there will probably be only two or
three to begin with—to undertake to meet in church
once a week at a suitable time, and pray together for
half an hour; or perhaps less than this at the beginning. At first, of course, the priest must take a leading part, help, suggest and perhaps instruct; and the
fact that, as the group develops, he will naturally ask
it to pray for particular things and persons, will
always keep him in close touch with it. But the
sooner these meetings pass into lay control, the
better. There will inevitably be much freedom and
variety as regards devotional methods and technique.
Some groups will generally prefer to pray together in
silence; some will like to use biddings, litanies, or
particular forms and acts of prayer. All this is of
secondary importance. The important thing is that
week by week there should be in the church this
homely concerted act of worship and waiting upon
God. The natural tendency of such groups to develop
into a mere intercessory guild must be carefully
guarded against. Worship, adoration, an increased
sense of the reality and attractiveness of God, a
deepening communion with Christ—these should be
their first concern. Intercession is not the side on
which most of our busy British prayers tend to fall
short, but adoration and self-offering. Yet powerful
and realistic intercessory action is always the work
of those in whom the Godward temper of adoration
and trust has first been established. There are plenty
of simple books of devotion, with suitable litanies,
acts and biddings which the group can take when
needed for guidance; and from time to time, a led
meditation, a simple picturing of a Gospel scene, and

acts of prayer and communion with Christ developed from and within that scene—in fact, an elementary form of the Ignatian meditation and colloquy—will be found unrivalled in its power of drawing the group more deeply into the spirit of prayer.

These groups need to be formed slowly and quietly, through personal contacts; but once established it is astonishing how quickly they become bound together, lose self-consciousness and shyness, begin to find new members and develop a corporate life of their own. If a group goes well, it will gradually become the nucleus of a network of prayer, spreading through the parish like leaven, deeply concerned with its life and problems, lifting up to God its anxieties, sorrows and sins. Into it can be drawn the invalids and old people; all those who cannot come to the church, but who can undertake to pray with the group at the agreed time in their own homes, and can be asked to remember its objects of prayer. In this way they are drawn into a living spiritual fellowship and released from loneliness; and are given an entirely new sense of sharing in the life and work of their church. All suffering can be transformed into prayer, and added to the Cross, and so given a new meaning and dignity; and here is one of the simplest ways in which this great spiritual truth can be taught.

In large congregations it ought to be possible to set going two such groups. One will consist of young people, who must be encouraged to conduct it in their own way, and whose religious life will gain enormously in realism and interest by the responsibility and mutual support which the group life entails. To it some at least of each year's confirmation candidates can be attached. The other group will consist of older men and women, of whom the first members will perhaps be found in the Parochial Church Council, Mothers' Union and C.E.M.S. After a time these groups will develop their own procedure and technique. Their existence will very soon make itself felt in the quality of the Sunday worship and in the changed atmosphere of the parish church; the intimidating bleakness which too often meets and baffles us being turned into homeliness, with the result that it will be more and more used for private prayer. The important thing is to preserve the note of free association, avoid the official tone, irksome rules, anything which stresses one particular type of churchmanship. Nor should membership be limited to regular communicants; the prayer group is rather a way of creating regular communicants. Even those who hardly go to church at other times should be welcomed if they wish to come. But the nucleus of the group must be faithful in their regularity of attendance; and take their responsibility as to this very seriously.

I was present some time ago at the Sunday morning service of a country church, where such a group had been established. When the service was over and the vicar had gone into the vestry, a woman in one of the pews started an act of thanksgiving, which was joined in by the rest. They sang a psalm, recited some simple acts of devotion, and the leader said a prayer. It was all simple, homely, natural; orderly and yet spontaneous: a real devotion of the people, setting their seal, as it were, on the worship which had been offered in their name. Where such a custom as this is set going, worship becomes a reality and the life of prayer will grow. Further, although intercession is never to be its first object, the praying group will become a powerful intercessory instrument. It will naturally tend to make its own the special interests of the parish, its problems and undertakings; and to hold up before God the sinful, the troubled, the sick. It is a humble bit of the Praying Church, lifting up hands towards the supernatural world, waiting upon God; and therefore shares in all the duties and the graces of the Praying Church. It should become, and can become, the spearhead of the spiritual life of the parish; a powerful redeeming and evangelizing force, supporting the ministry and exercising an influence the more profound because it is secret. Within such groups individuals will gradually learn more and more of what prayer can be; and this combination of the corporate and the personal spiritual life, praying as members of the church, aware of their social responsibility and yet also as individual souls most dear to God, is, I am sure, what we should aim at if we want to make strong and sane Christians and not merely devotees.

Finally, though we have humbly to confess that all true prayer is caused by God and is a response to His incitement, and therefore that we are entirely unable of ourselves to teach others to pray or cause them to pray—except to some extent by suggestion and demonstration—still, it is clear that we can help their response, wake up their sense of spiritual reality, and stop various sources of error by teaching them in the right way about prayer. For that purpose it is surely important to have in our minds some general conception of its character and place in human experience. Even on the simplest lines, for example, when instructing confirmation candidates, we ought ever to keep in the foreground the fact that prayer is not some separate devotional activity, but a part of the whole life; the bringing of all life, every bit of daily work and every human relationship, into harmony with God's Will, and glorifying Him in it. Therefore it will include not only the praise of God, and petitions to God, but spiritual work done for and with God, as members of the Church. This conception of prayer as something positive and dynamic—a Godward activity in which our whole being is involved, in which we do work—is far more likely to arouse interest and enthusiasm, especially in young people, than any emphasis on its devotional side alone. It has something to say to the vigorous and the young, who want, and rightly want, a part to play in the creative action of their faith; and something also to say to the physically helpless, the sick and the old, who can yet make a great contribution to the Church's life of prayer, not only in the way of definite intercession, but by a giving of their whole will and love, their trials and sufferings, to His mysterious purposes, to be used as He wills for other souls.

In Père Charles's beautiful *Prayer for all Times* there is a passage in which he says to a soul which has been delivered from some sin or danger, or been brought from darkness to light, "How do you know whose prayer it is which has prevailed before God and won you this grace? Perhaps it is that old beggar at the church door, or the applewoman in the market, or some sleepless sufferer, or some little child; who made with simplicity an offering of their prayer, and it was accepted for the purposes of God." That is a doctrine which, put in a simple form, can and should enter into the teaching of prayer to the laity. It means that everything can be brought into the atmosphere of worship, offered to God and so turned into prayer. Especially, for example, it should be possible to teach confirmation candidates that, in being received into full Church membership and given full Church privileges, they also accept full Church responsibilities. This includes taking their part in the Church's great redeeming life of prayer; a duty to be performed regularly, not for themselves, but as members of the Household of Faith, loyally taking their share in the household work, whatever their own feelings and preferences may happen to be.

All real prayer can be brought under the three heads of adoration of God, communion with God, co-operation with God; and of these adoration, worship, the lifting up of heart and mind to the Eternal, should always be taught first. Many people say that this is difficult, that in practice petition comes more naturally and is easier to explain. But if we begin with self-interest, or even with our neighbours' or the world's interests, we may never get any further. "Lift up your hearts" is the formula for Christian prayer. It seeks first the Kingdom of God; and we ought to keep that truth in the foreground. We can show what adoration is, by the direct method; by the use of the great adoring prayers of Christianity, such as the *Gloria* and the *Sanctus*, or by simple acts of faith, hope and charity, which are charged with the spirit of worship and love, and so are able to evoke that spirit in those who use them. That which we do in prayer has its subjective effect and importance. It speaks to God, and speaks to our own souls too; and the acts of adoration and trust in which the priest makes his people join, will tend far more effectually than any exhortation or description to open their souls to the supernatural and produce in them adoration and trust. No instruction on prayer should ever end without the practising together of the kind of prayer which has been taught.

As regards the teaching of intercession, it is surely of the first importance that this great spiritual act should be made real to those who do it; avoiding in the first instance large, vague petitions and world-causes, and beginning with the most homely and immediate interests and needs. Until people have learned to love their neighbours, fellow workers, village or town, and hold these and their needs up to God, it is useless and unreal to encourage them to launch into the great intercessory efforts which are needed if they are really, and not formally, to hold up to God in love the needs of the world.

Further, we should surely insist more than we commonly do on the close connection between prayer and sacrifice; and plainly denounce that too common type of prayer which asks for results to which those who pray are not prepared to make any real contribution. It is not easy to justify at the bar of reality the prayers for peace and for reunion which are now offered in countless churches, and by numerous individuals who are not in fact prepared to do one difficult thing, or to make a single sacrifice either of possessions or of prejudices, in the interests of peace or of reunion. Peace is very costly, and reunion will be very costly. Both will need great renunciation; a great acceptance of the Cross. To tell people to pray for either is unreal, unless we also tell them such prayer carries its own sacrificial obligation; and those who offer it must be prepared to take their share of effort, and pay their share of the cost. So, too, with other more immediate interests—unemployment, industrial problems, missions—about which Church people are encouraged to put up frequent petitions, but often do not exert themselves much. Our teaching on prayer would gain immensely in reality and power, and be taken more seriously by many who now ignore it, did we emphasize the intimate connection between prayer and our action outside prayer, and the unworthiness of mere cadging demands that God will do things which really lie within our own responsibility. Young people, who instinctively recoil from unreality, and to whom the generous, the heroic, the creative make a strong appeal, can quickly be made to see this point; and learn to regard Christian action and Christian prayer as inseparable parts of one whole.

In conclusion, there is the question of the personal instruction and advice on the interior life of prayer, its deeper aspects and problems, which the priest may at any time be asked to give to individuals; the guidance and support of a soul seeking closer communion with God. That, I suppose, is the most delicate and responsible work with which anyone can be entrusted; for here we are moving in regions where we often know ourselves to be insecure, and may be asked for help by those who are already far beyond us in spirituality. The only real safeguards are a great and confident submission to God as His servants, and great humility as regards ourselves and our own ideas. Patience, moderation and lightness of touch, a consistent resistance of the temptation to press souls on, carefulness in not giving advanced books to those who are not yet ready for them, or in any other way trying to go faster than the Holy Spirit, are of the first importance. The growth of a soul in prayer is generally a very gradual process; and attempts to introduce it into regions to which it has not yet been called by God can do nothing but harm.

It is always by the faithful and humble practice of the prayer now possible to it, and not by making spiritual experiments, that the soul is prepared for further advance.

There are two outstanding and opposite dangers which await the modern priest called to the direction of souls. One is peculiar to our own times; the knowledge—seldom very deep—of the psychology of religion which is now at the disposal of most people interested in the spiritual life. This often induces an unduly critical attitude towards the imaginative and emotional types of religious experience; which are, after all, common to humanity, and, however close their connection with the purely natural levels of our life, can yet be the medium of a real communion with God. The imaginative type of devotion ought not to be condemned out of hand, because we think that we recognize its obvious psychological origins. To do this would be to discount some of the most life-giving experiences of the Saints. But, on the other hand, neither should it be regarded as the sign of a special holiness. Like all else in the life of prayer, it must be judged by its fruits; and allowed to go on so long, and only so long, as it produces an increase of humility, courage and love.

The other danger to which the modern director is exposed is worse. It is the inclination to discover a possible mystic in everyone who develops a passive or otherwise unusual type of prayer, or lays claim to visionary or other abnormal experiences. The general reading of mystical literature has produced a great crop of this kind of self-deception; often unwittingly encouraged by clergy who know themselves to be inexperienced in these matters, and are too humble-minded to deal with them by the obvious standards of common sense. All those who are called to personal work with souls know the type to whom his or her—I am afraid usually her—devotional life appears of paramount importance, and who is willing to talk about it at great length. The genuine contemplative is seldom found in this class. Those who are really moving towards deeper states of prayer will probably be those who make the least demands on their clergy, and are not at all anxious to be understood; quiet and humble souls who have not much to say about themselves. These can be helped much by encouragement and support in the periods of darkness and dryness which are certain to come upon them, and by guarding them against the constant risk of spiritual overstrain. In all this, of course, some first-hand knowledge of the great Christian writers on prayer—not the dilute account of their teaching now given in a multitude of little books—will help; and this is the knowledge which, plainly, every priest ought to possess as a necessary part of his equipment. But his greatest help in this personal work with souls, in fact, his only real source of light and strength, will be his own life of communion with God. In Him all souls are interconnected; and it is in his times of prayer—even when this prayer seems most difficult and arid—that the priest will be mysteriously taught the needs and spiritual state of those whom he is called to help. So we end where we began. The work of the parish priest, for God and for souls, depends for its worth, and depends wholly, on his own life of prayer.

VIII

THE TEACHER'S VOCATION

An Address to Teachers of Religion[1]

WHEN I was in the North this year, I was present at some sheep-dog trials. That seems perhaps an odd subject to introduce in an address to teachers. But, after all, there is something analogous to the sheep-dog's vocation in the sort of work that Sunday-school teachers are trying to do. You are all trying to help the shepherds of souls to deal with the lambs and young sheep of the flock. For in all religious teaching, it is that pastoral and personal work with souls which matters; you have undertaken a little bit of pastoral work.

Now those sheep-dogs that afternoon gave me a much better address on the way in which pastoral work among souls should be done than I shall be able to give you. They were helping the shepherd to deal with a lot of very active sheep and lambs, to persuade them into the right pastures, to keep them from rushing down the wrong paths. And how did the successful dog do it? Not by barking, fuss, ostentatious authority, any kind of busy behaviour. The best dog that I saw never barked once; and he spent an astonishing amount of his time sitting perfectly still, looking at the shepherd. The communion of spirit between them was perfect. They worked as a

[1] An address given at the Annual Meeting of the Southwark Diocesan Sunday School Association in the Church House, 1927 Published by St. Christopher Press, 1928.

157

unit. Neither of them seemed anxious or in a hurry. Neither was committed to a rigid plan; they were always content to wait. That dog was the docile and faithful agent of another mind. He used his whole intelligence and initiative, but always in obedience to his master's directive will; and was ever prompt at self-effacement. The little mountain sheep he had to deal with were amazingly tiresome, as expert in doubling and twisting and going the wrong way as any naughty little boy. The dog went steadily on with it; and his tail never ceased to wag.

What did that mean? It meant that his relation to the shepherd was the centre of his life; and because of that, he enjoyed doing his job with the sheep, he did not bother about the trouble, nor get discouraged with the apparent results. The dog had transcended mere dogginess. His actions were dictated by something right beyond himself. He was the agent of the shepherd, working for a scheme which was not his own and the whole of which he could not grasp; and it was just that which was the source of the delightedness, the eagerness, and also the discipline with which he worked. But he would not have kept that peculiar and intimate relation unless he had sat down and looked at the shepherd a good deal.

Now it is much the same here, isn't it? Does not your work, as teachers, trainers of young people, if it is to be well and effectively done, ultimately stand or fall by the quality of your invisible attachments? For though it is work much bigger than ourselves, since the whole future of all the souls you touch is wrapped up in it; yet we all know that the strain, difficulty and discouragement of it are often great. It may have to be done in depressing and monotonous surroundings, and you can hardly help getting weary and mechanical unless you take it in the sheep-dog's spirit; that is, unless you make and keep your relation to God the most real and vivid factor in your life; letting all details of your work fall into place as a part of the landscape of which He is the governing and all-irradiating fact. A vivid and realistic faith in the Reality of God, an absolute hope in Him and in the ultimate triumph of His purpose for each soul—however unlikely it may sometimes seem—a burning love which ignores, or even welcomes, difficulties and discouragement: that is the only possible temper of soul in which such work as yours can be well done.

That means, of course, that only the supernatural virtues of faith, hope and charity can help you to train and to keep your pupils in the Christian life. We might retranslate these three words as Vision, Confidence and Generosity—the supreme qualities needed by those who work in souls. The sheep in the Bible image follow the shepherd. He goes first, and tries each bit of the way before they come to it. He looks ahead, knows where he is leading them: Vision. He is quite sure of the way: Confidence. He adapts himself to their pace, gives himself without stint to their requirements: Generosity. And all who work under Him need these qualities too.

What do we mean by this faith, this vision? Don't we mean simply spiritual realism: the seeing of all things in the spiritual light; seeing the whole world and all the men and women in it, all the children and young people who are your special care, only in their relation to God? How utterly life is changed in the hours in which we do attain to something of that vision! In the light of it we see that we are put into a world of living, growing things, and it is

our immense privilege to help some of them to grow
up towards God. Now, we cannot do that properly
unless we have a clear view of what we are aiming at;
and that is why Vision, the fruit of prayer, becomes
a first duty of all teachers. Why we must give ourselves space, leisure and tranquillity, to look as well
as we can at God and His world of souls. A man's
or woman's view of reality is the one really important
thing about them. It enters into and conditions all
we think, do and are. It colours all we can give to the
world. And when we come to religion, which deals
with the Reality of all realities; how transcendently
important it is that our outlook should be large and
free, yet humbly loving and creaturely, recognizing
the depth as well as the width of our Christian faith!
That means that our own secret and inward life towards God is an important part, in fact the most
important part of the work we are called upon to do
for Him; and that this secret life must have at its
heart a spirit of adoring contemplation, the sort of
prayer in which we turn towards God in and for
Himself. Only so far as we are able to keep that
attitude will we keep sufficient courage and eagerness
to meet and conquer the disheartening aspects of our
job.

What, then, is this job? Surely as Christians we
must consider that it is to co-operate with God in
rearing up certain souls which are to form cells of
the Body of Christ. And the true object of this whole
process is not merely the teaching, the training, the
improvement or even the saving of those young and
growing souls; excellent as all this may be. Your
ideal is not just to make your young people good
citizens, or good Anglicans. That's not nearly good
enough. The real object is the glory of God. *That*

is the vision which is to stand ever before you as you go about your work. That sublime overruling aim, not any humanitarian end alone, is the true source of your confidence and generous self-giving. Heaven and earth are full of Thy glory: I have a chance of adding a bit to that. It is difficult to see this sometimes in our great cities. Nevertheless, everything you do, say or think which lies in the direction of God only has meaning, as a contribution to that glory. The *Sanctus* must be the perpetual and classic prayer of all who attempt to work in souls.

It follows from all this that the most important thing for you is your vision, your sense, of that God whom your work must glorify. The richer, deeper, wider, truer your vision of Divine Reality the more real, rich and fruitful your work is going to be. You must feel the mysterious attraction of God, His loveliness and wonder, if you are ever going—in however simple a way—to impart it to others. And the next thing you want, and want badly, is that spirit of confidence which is the mainstay of hope. The quiet certainty that God's purpose will prevail in spite of appearances to the contrary; the loyal dog's conviction that sooner or later somehow those sheep *are* going to be got in.

Here perhaps the first thing is to get firmly into our minds, that the only doer of all our work is always God Himself. You and I are simply small tools of different kinds which He picks up and uses, and through which the moulding and shaping of men's souls is done. Hence, however successful we may sometimes seem to be, or however fruitless some of our best efforts appear, there is nothing in that either to flatter self-love or to induce despair. You were just the chisel or bit of sandpaper that happened

L

to be suitable at that stage for that special bit of work. Someone else may finish it later on. The boy, the girl, go away. Perhaps you never see them again. God goes on with them. Perhaps puts them aside for a time; perhaps takes another method, another tool.

How, then, are you going to think of the Power and Love which thus takes and uses you? Surely in the deepest, richest, humblest, most loving and adoring way of which you are capable; refusing the lazy inclination to rest in religious phrases, remembering the overplus of God's reality and glory beyond anything our little minds can conceive. Such an awed sense of His greatness will not mean religious dreaminess or loftiness. It will make you better, not less efficient, teachers of simple things.

Do you remember how, in Thomas Hardy's *Far from the Madding Crowd*, Gabriel Oak, that perfect shepherd, used to stand upon a hill at night and gaze into the starry sky, until he could feel this little world rolling through the immensity of space? That great vision made him a better shepherd, not a worse one. When Bathsheba's sheep over-ate themselves and got indigestion, he was the person who was sent for and knew exactly what to do. And so too it is with the teacher. If you once allowed yourself to think that your immediate job was everything, and nothing lay beyond to give it meaning, you might soon give up in disgust, when petty worries and failures overwhelmed you. But if beyond that little bit of life you can glimpse the steadfast reality of God, and feel that same living and infinite reality penetrating and moulding all souls and working through you, then you gain new heart for going on. It is towards an ever greater sense of that Eternal

Reality that you want to help your pupils' souls to grow. You want them to expand and become more and more what human life is really meant to be, to move on from an existence bound down to natural things and desires, into an existence that is controlled by spiritual needs and desires. But if you are to do that successfully, you must have and keep something of the vision that you are trying to impart.

So it is in and through your work, which sometimes you may be tempted to look upon as mostly a matter of moral training, or of teaching the routine practice of the religious life, that your own secret spiritual life, your steadfastly held vision of God, your loving self-surrender as His tools, is going to justify itself and prove its quality. It will be the decisive factor in that which you give the children and young people with whom you deal. For their sakes you are called upon to sanctify yourselves; and for the strengthening of this life you must use to the utmost all those channels, those aids, through which God comes to you. The rich and complex variety of reading, meditation, prayer and sacraments, the power of rightly used liturgic offices; these feed your minds and hearts with suitable suggestions and keep your thoughts and feelings within the atmosphere of God. By the balanced use of all these means you must go on and on, widening, deepening, enriching your concept of Him; gaining not so much a new as a renewed vision, which keeps and illuminates afresh all the elements of your faith.

We have thought of the vision of God which you should try to keep and get in your work; but there is another side to your problem. The ideal sheep-dog is not always looking at the shepherd. He also keeps a very keen eye on the sheep. What about that?

What is to be your vision of the children and young people to whom you are sent? Once again, nothing but the best is worth while. You need an outlook on human souls which shall regard each as a unique and living spirit infinitely dear to God; a child of the celestial nursery having a latent tendency to Him of a particular kind, which you have the chance of fostering and helping to grow. This, when we look round at the average members of a Sunday school or class, may seem an extreme way of putting things. Yet it is really the only possible way for you, as Christians, to regard your work. That complete confidence in God which is the fruit of a life of prayer brings with it a certain power of seeing all His children from the supernatural point of view; as little growing spirits whose angels stand before Him. The widespreading love and compassion which has no doubts or reserves—an intimate, generous belief in souls of all sorts and an infinite desire to help them to grow right—this is surely to love human creatures in the way in which God loves the world. That means keeping your eye all the time on the real, the spiritual creature; its possibilities, its innate need of God, its difficulties and weakness, yet its wonderful and touching beauty: a beauty so wonderful and touching that it could carry the values of the Incarnation. It means that you look upon your vocation mainly as a call to cherish and feed your pupils, help their growth towards holiness. In fact, wise *feeding* of the young and growing souls given into your care is, I suppose, the main part of your work.

What is feeding? It is bringing to a living, growing and organic creature something from outside itself; which it can take in and digest and turn into part of its own substance, and so grow and maintain its energy. Feeding means gathering material, and so preparing it that it suits the appetite, digestion and needs of each of those in your care. It will mean keeping in personal touch with all that is best and most living in religion; so that you may have plenty of fresh nourishing food to give, and not have to fall back on tinned stuff. It means that what you give in words, acts, suggestion or influence is of infinite importance, and no trouble is too much to get it right. That may involve giving up many of your private prejudices; always thinking of your pupils, rather than of your own point of view. It means an elastic hold upon everything except essentials; and also a very clear idea of those essentials on which you must never lose your grasp.

The next point is that your classes do not consist of little angels, by any manner of means. They consist of human beings; who are bodies *and* spirits, whose physical being is the result of organic evolution, and who have got to live in a world which is material and spiritual both at once. Our Lord did not say to St. Peter: "Instruct My angels." He said: "Feed My sheep . . . feed My lambs"; a much more rough-and ready, homely, earthly sort of job. What are these sheep and lambs? They are units, consisting, as we say, of soul and body; but of soul and body so closely locked together that we cannot safely think of one without the other, or disregard the fact that they are profoundly influencing one another all the time. So, though you must never look upon your job as merely humanitarian and ethical; still less must you look on it as purely spiritual, quite unconnected with outward bodily life. Certainly it often seems as though the body pulls one way and the soul another way. The animal and the spiritual creature have conflicting interests and desires. But it is your business to try to resolve that conflict; to help those in your charge, as we say, to sublimate the great animal instincts and desires. No believer in an incarnational religion who is called upon to deal with souls can afford for one minute to disregard the bodily life with all its opportunities and dangers. You are dealing with creatures immersed in organic life, who take colour from their surroundings and express themselves in physical no less than mental ways. Creatures whose psychic life is so intricately entwined with their bodily life that even character itself is deeply affected by the body's chemical state and the activities of its glands. That is the material handed out to you, which you must help to grow up towards God; and that too is the sort of creatures you are yourselves. Look those facts squarely in the face, and be ready for their often disconcerting results. Do not allow yourselves to dwell in a spiritual dreamland remote from actual life, or sink to the merely naturalistic view of our strangely compounded human personality which psychology invites us to accept. Psychology is a splendid servant for those who work in souls; but a very bad master. We have to keep it in its place.

What next? Having this general vision of those in your care, as being at once, so to speak, the children of the natural world and the children of the spiritual world, living in time yet with a capacity for eternity; what are you to think of first? Surely you should think first: Here is, not a childish soul for me to squeeze into the Anglican mould, but a living, growing thing, which has a certain implanted tendency and should grow up to a certain fulfilment. And I can help that process if I faithfully bring to bear my intelligence as well as my love. So, what kind of creature is it? What is its type? No use treating it as a delphinium if, as a matter of fact, it is a baby carrot. The differences in souls are innumerable; and some of what the old writers called discernment of spirits is an absolute essential to you, if you are to avoid mortifying and even dangerous mistakes with your pupils. Each child who comes really into touch with you, represents an opportunity to train, to educate, to help to produce and make effective another labourer for the vineyard; and in giving such training you must consider the type of each. In dealing with boys and girls, wise parents and teachers have in their minds the ideal man or woman they want to help them to be. Not a rigid type, but a sort of classic standard of well-being and general rightness; within which each human type can fulfil itself. The educator who is able to hold on to the pattern while treating each separate child on its own lines is the one who succeeds in making men and women who are of value to the society in which they are placed.

Don't you think the same is true in your work? Side by side with each particular pupil, who may be willing and responsible, or may be tiresome, dull, difficult and selfish, stands the Christian universal, the all-inclusive model, towards which you have the privilege of helping that particular child to grow. You are taking part in the Church's great job, the sublimation of human nature, the production of Christ-likeness in different ways and degrees in human creatures of all sorts and different types; or rather the freeing of the channels along which grace can enter and effect this transformation, this growth in souls.

I suppose everyone here knows what it is to see a soul that has got the Christian look; the peace and tranquillity of an engine which is running right instead of out of gear, the unmistakable radiance from within overwhelming the hardness and bitterness of a self-occupied spirit at odds with life. To see that is, I suppose, one of the most convincing and exhilarating experiences in the world; and you can prepare the way for it to happen. You will probably find, in so far as you have been able to do this, that it was not your careful teaching, discipline and training which made possible this wondrous change. It is far more likely to have been some chance suggestion, some word which you hardly recalled, which began the work; a word that you were only able to say because of the faithfulness of your own life.

If we study the lives of great religious teachers—and that is a very fruitful sort of study for you—one thing we can hardly fail to learn from them is how gentle, gradual and patient is the way in which they do this work. The nearer those who teach religion are to God, the more they seem to share His long patience and compassionate, cherishing, unexacting attitude to men; and where the Holy Spirit takes and uses any individual for the work of teaching souls, He will always bring their method nearer and nearer to this gentleness. I don't pretend this sort of way of tackling your work will be easy. It requires indeed a perpetual death to self. Everyone here must have experience of the fact that teaching children and adolescents can be an intensely tiresome job. But perhaps it helps us if we remember that it is God Himself who comes to us, in and with even the most tiresome young creatures. That which His Spirit has given to them is in need of something which that same Spirit has given to us. Buried in each of those souls—sometimes not easy to discover—is a particular tendency; which, properly fostered, is going to make them useful to God. *You* have got to find that tendency; help, support and feed it. What a responsibility, and what an honour!

If, then, from one point of view, your work means taking your place by the side of the shepherd and sharing as nearly as you can his outlook on the sheep; from another, it means taking your place by the side of each of those different sheep, trying to share and understand their limited outlook, and thus humbly learning the way in which you can help them best. While on the one hand you want to lead them deeper and deeper into the wonderful joy and interestingness of religion, make their lives as full and rich as ever you can; on the other hand you have got to teach and encourage them to find spiritual food where they are—in the paths of common life, where most of their time is going to be spent. I think it is because young people are not taught more to find God here, recognize Him in ordinary life, that many fail to find Him at all. Therefore you must teach your little flock to find the food of their souls as they go along the highroad. You must first find it there yourself, and then teach them to take it. If you ever let yourself think that the religious turnips and things which you chop up and administer in the Sunday school or class are the only spiritual food of the flock, and God only feeds them in that particular way; then, under the exacting and largely irreligious conditions of modern life, you are going to make a very bad job of their training and nourishment, and must not be surprised if a lot of them wander away and look elsewhere for food. They ought to learn from you to get as much of the heavenly food of Eternal Life from nibbling the ordinary grass on the edge of the road, as they do from the special feeding of the Church. You want them to find there the savour and presence of God; because you know as a matter of fact that He is in those daily events, joys and pains of their lives. Therefore you should make it your business to turn those ordinary things of life into spiritual food for the souls you teach.

Most of the children who are committed to you will grow up to busy, driven lives. They look forward to incessant work, among concrete responsibilities, anxieties and interests. They are not going to be people with special powers of spiritual devotion, able to use long periods of prayer, even if they had time for them. Hence it is very important to make them realize now that the Christian communion with God takes many different forms; that there is no outward act, no kind of work, no drudgery, joy, suffering, which cannot be turned into a means of intercourse, a virtual prayer, provided it is accepted from the hand of God in a spirit of love; that He can and will come to them incessantly in the tram and the office, the shop, the factory, the home; perpetually offering something which, faithfully accepted, will become real food for their souls. It is your greatest privilege to teach your children to recognize this. Teach them the fact of God's mysterious nearness, and of His constant sheltering, moulding, strengthening, feeding Presence with each separate life.

And last, what about the sacred privilege and duty which is yours, of serving your pupils in purely spiritual ways? Here we are touching the fringe of mysteries which lie right beyond us: the way in which one human spirit can by its love and prayer touch and change another human spirit; can lift a soul into the atmosphere of God.

God's creative and transforming action does not seem to work upon human life as something separate from the souls of men and women. It mostly works in and through the souls of men and women; and you offered yourselves for this purpose when you undertook pastoral work. As He uses our bodies and minds, acts through them to transform and to improve the physical world—so He uses our spirits for His saving and creative work. Therefore your secret inner life, your dedicated will and love, your prayers, your renunciations, may be the instruments through which the growing souls of your pupils are helped best. Perhaps the most real and enduring of the work you do for them will be that which you do in the hiddenness of your soul. It is a living tool, which works in the world of prayer. It can be a genuine distributing centre of God's creative power. Hence each time you take one of these children into your prayer, you are accepting unconditionally a direct piece of spiritual work. Again, what an honour and what a responsibility! Does it not then become your first duty to keep your own inner life strong and healthy; in order that it may be able to do this, the most sacred part of the work to which you are called?

IX

THE SPIRITUAL LIFE OF THE TEACHER[1]

I WANT to talk to you this afternoon about the hidden side—or better still, the hidden foundations—of that life to which you have all been called in one form or another: the life of a teacher. For every full human life, of course, has two sides: its relation to the Eternal God, the Changeless Reality on whom it depends; and its relation to the changing world, and especially the changing human beings among whom it is placed. It is the first of these relationships, the deep and hidden intercourse with the unchanging God, which gives to human life its dignity, meaning and peace; and it is of this that I am going to speak.

Well, at first sight, it seems, doesn't it? as though the inner life of the teacher, her relation with God, must be much the same as that of any other Christian. That is to say, its three great marks must be, first, a steady and humble worship of God in Himself, His beauty and His perfection; next, a ceaseless, loving self-giving to Him; and last, the effort to serve and co-operate with Him. But if we consider it a little more deeply, we realize that there is something peculiar to the position of a teacher, which requires a

[1] An address delivered to the South London Centre of the Guild of the Epiphany. Evelyn Underhill appended this note: "This address, which incorporates material that I have used on other occasions, was not written for publication; but is now printed for the convenience of those members of the Guild of the Epiphany who were not able to be present when it was given."

special quality in the interior and spiritual life that supports it.

You, a Child of God, are specially called upon to help and train the younger children of God to understand and deal with the rich and many-levelled life in which He has placed them: to educate them, in the fullest, most profoundly Christian sense of that ill-used word. So, a right attitude to Him, the satisfying of your inner need of Him, matters in your case supremely; not merely on account of yourselves and your own souls, but—which is much more important —on account of those who have been put in your charge, the little growing spirits for whom you are responsible to God. If that inner life goes wrong, your work goes wrong. You, so small and weak, are to show them their way about, in a life that only has meaning because it is created and loved and guided by God. How can you hope to do that, unless your own sense of His reality is very strong and humble and realistic—full of awe and full of joy? Your secret life of prayer, and your share in the great life of the Church, must nourish this: keep you in His atmosphere, and so give you peace within your work and power to do it. A deep, wide and steady devotional life, pursued up hill and down dale, in darkness and in light, whether you feel like it or whether you don't, is therefore the essential foundation of your teaching work. In neglecting to gain this, and keep it, you are neglecting the most important aspect of that work—failing God. This is obvious, isn't it?

And first, just because that dangerous word Teacher is used to you and about you, your whole inner life must be ruled and sweetened by a ceaseless teachableness; a sense of subordination to God, in all things both little and great. For you are simply one particular dispenser of a little trickle of His Infinite Light and Love. Whether you are actually teaching religion or not, your work is always religious; because it is concerned with explaining God's Universe, its laws and action and beauty, and all the behaviour and discoveries of His creatures, and the right use of the bodies and minds He has made. If you follow out the meaning of what you are doing, you will find it all leads back to Him: for He is the one Reality, the Fountain of all life. And so, once again, keeping your own attitude to Him healthy, alert, humble, is a first charge on your time. We often speak of the teacher's vocation: but a vocation does not mean that we do the calling and choosing, it means that God calls and chooses. And that call should be the beginning of a lifelong correspondence with Him: often of course entailing quite a lot of trouble and effort on our part, as all great things do, but the essential condition of your work. For in that work, if it is worth anything, you continually give yourself: and you must receive and go on receiving, if you are to give and go on giving. Your whole life hangs on a great Givenness. And so the more your life is ruled by a humble and docile dependence on God the more, that is to say, it becomes in its totality a Prayer, the more useful you will be to Him and to those who are placed in your care. You will then be an actual link between His Creative Love and the children you teach. No lesser ideal than that is worth while for you, as Christians, is it? And that means that your whole lives must be coloured by your loving attention to God. For He has chosen you for a job which, properly done, would bit by bit transform and save the world. The soul of every child, says Péguy, represents a hope of God. He has committed to you some of His hope. What a privilege, isn't it? What a meaning it must give to your life; and how obvious it is that this tremendous vocation must govern your whole life of prayer! And this is what I want to talk about this afternoon.

The life of prayer is so great and various there is something in it for everyone. It is like a garden which grows everything, from alpines to potatoes. Or again, it is like that ocean of God in which St. Gregory said that elephants can swim and lambs can paddle. Even a baby can do something about it. No saint has exhausted its possibilities yet. What is there here specially for you as teachers? What ought to be the ruling disposition, so to speak, that governs your life of prayer in all its ups and downs, joys and difficulties and problems, light and shade, and variousness? Isn't it just this? I have been brought into my present position by God: in order that, in a particular way, I may be useful to Him. My little life, which I began perhaps by thinking so important, is to be more and more hidden in the great tide of His infinite life. My tiny activities whatever they are —teaching, or cherishing, some of His other children —only matter because they are part of His great spendthrift, saving, loving action within life. Through me He can touch, mould, create, transform other spirits. I was given to Him in baptism—and I gave myself to Him again of my own free will—just for that.

So my prayer is not any longer, or ever again, to be the separate prayer of a tight little ring-fenced soul. It is not a self-cultivating, self-exploring job; nor is it a mere duet, however fervent, between me and God, The spiritual life of the Christian Church is not a series of duets: it is a great symphony, in which every soul has a part, and no soul is independent of the rest. My prayer is to be the prayer of a living member of that Church; a ceaseless self-giving to God for His purpose, and ceaseless accepting from Him of all I need to carry out that purpose. The altar, the place of oblation, where I give myself without limit to God as a reasonable and living sacrifice, and thereby receive from Him new life; the whole drive of my devotional life should be towards that.

This means learning and practising ever more faithfully and completely those three movements which make up the full life of our souls: (1) an adoring, unconditional and absolutely trustful self-giving to God; (2) a drawing near, to have communion with Him in meditation and silence, when our own action ceases, and His action renews and feeds us; and last and best, that co-operation in which we become His actual tools and channels, because there is an open path between His generous Spirit and our small dependent spirits. So these are the three movements which are to go with you in your worship and secret prayers and work, however exacting, practical and apparently unspiritual that work may seem to be: or hardest of all, when your lives seem to be filled with an unprofitable routine. When the lambs won't eat the food you have got ready for them, when you are worn out by their restlessness or discouraged by their slowness—all that, every bit of it, is for you part of one devoted life of prayer: lit by adoration, sweetened by communion and braced by the sense of co-operation with God, who has put these little spirits in your care and made you responsible for them. You cannot afford to leave any of those three movements out, if you want your inner life to be balanced, fruitful and sane. We find them all twined together in the prayers of the saints. "What shall I say my God, my Holy Joy," says St. Augustine. That is the first movement. "O knit my soul unto thee!" says the Psalmist, and thousands after him. That is the second movement. "Take me and use me, as your most humble tool, for the good of souls—for your service," says Elisabeth Leseur, the modern saint. That is the third movement.

Take me and use me, as a tool. I have taken my place in God's workshop as a bit of His creative apparatus. So I must keep myself at His disposal, and respond with humble love, as He teaches me from within and shows me His will. "So teach us to number our days that we may apply our hearts unto Wisdom": that is what we ought to ask, and go on asking. That we may stand by Thee, the Divine Wisdom, and know and love and help Thy creation— or whatever bit of Thy creation is given us to care for and love and work at—with that selfless knowledge, and that disinterested love, free from all claimfulness, which does not conflict with Thy holy knowledge and love.

That is what we have to do, isn't it? apply our hearts, our energy, our whole selves, not merely our heads, to the Wisdom of God. Not in order to get nice religious feelings for ourselves; but in order to enter with Him into life, learn to look at it with the eyes of the Artist Creator, see it as it really is, with its beauty and nobleness, and its sorrow, sin, weakness and dreariness—and then, serve it, help it, teach it, give ourselves for it. Apply our hearts in our meditations to His presence and His beauty; and then draw all life, and especially the bit we deal with, into

M

the circle of Charity, till we see that too in the light of His presence and His beauty.

Now we learn to see the whole texture of our life in that way—all the apparently unspiritual and tiresome children, all the organizations and activities, all the dull bits and disappointing bits—that takes some doing. It means getting the very flavour of the supernatural, the glow of Divine Love into our everyday routine; a sort of rhythm established in our souls by which everything as it comes along is lifted up towards God and seen in His light. This rhythm, this discipline, is what we must learn more and more in our secret prayers: resisting the temptation merely to try and enjoy God. We have to remember all the time that the real point is not the use we make of Him but the use He is making of us. For that we go into training, for that we sink our own secret longing for spiritual consolations; quite willing, because we really love Him, to go hungry and thirsty if needs be, and out of our devotional poverty make many rich.

Your life, inward and outward, as I see it, has got to be like one of those beautiful shot materials in which the gold thread runs one way and the coloured thread runs the other way, and both together make a fabric more beautiful than each would make alone; a fabric which has a certain lowly likeness to the stuff of our Lord's own life, because woven of ceaseless loving communion with God, and ceaseless teaching, helping and healing of men. Now our work is a side of the Christian life that is pretty clear to all of us. There the world is, with all kinds of things needing to be done; and here we are, obviously under orders to do what we can, in our particular job. But the other side of the Christian life, those golden threads of humble and loving worship which ought to run through the whole fabric, how much spiritual education we all need before we can weave in those threads evenly; so that the shimmer of eternity is seen beautifying the whole stuff of our working days! It means really applying our hearts unto wisdom—all the hoarded wisdom and experience of the Church, of our spiritual ancestors—if we are to learn to do that well. It means a firm determination to clear out at the very beginning all petty, sentimental, self-occupied notions of prayer; learning to see ourselves all the time as servants and fellow-workers, not as pets. Perhaps some of you have read *Dr. Doolittle's Circus*, a book which is nearly as full of spiritual wisdom as *Alice in Wonderland*. There is, you remember, one admirable member of the circus; a most steady and responsible creature called Sophy the Wise Seal. But unfortunately Sophy had a husband, whose name was Slushy. Now in the spiritual life Sophy is one of the best and most reliable of companions; but we have to keep a very sharp look-out for Slushy. He has his pious moments, when he tries to push his quiet wife on one side and suggest to us what a helpful animal he is—such a good appearance, so fervent, and so full of feeling. But Slushy, like all sentimentalists, is really a very self-indulgent creature. What he calls zest is mostly feverishness; and what he calls worship is mostly basking. There are some devotional books in which one seems to hear nothing but Slushy flapping his tail; just as in others the quiet wise Sophy finds a few humble words, which yet convey her utter submission to God. Slushy, though at first sight very attractive, with his warm devotional colour and soft fur, is really wrapped up in nothing better than his own feelings. Sophy may not have such a good coat; but she keeps in much better condition, because she looks at herself and her own feelings very little, and at God and the mighty purposes of God and the needs of the Children of God a very great deal. It is by keeping company with Sophy, sharing her point of view and sense of proportion, that we shall achieve a deep, healthy, self-forgetful inner life.

Again we are led back to self-oblivious adoration as the right colour of our worship: a lifting up of our eyes in loving admiration to the hills from whence cometh our strength. I think all we who dare to teach, even in the simplest way, should say every day the Collect for the sixth Sunday after Trinity: "Pour into our hearts such love . . . "—such generous, delighted devotedness to thee—"that we, loving Thee above all things, may obtain Thy promises." Loving *Thee* above all things—God in His Reality—if we do that, the other part will happen; but not otherwise. So here, the very foundation of the teacher's inner life is stated in unmistakable language. God first, adoration first, a passionate unconditional devotion to His purposes, His splendour, His reality: everything done in and for Him. An adoring adherence is to be the governing mood of your prayer; such a total and absolute devotion as can only come, be poured in, from the Spirit of Absolute Love—God. His interests are to be your interests, annihilating all concern with your personal status, personal success, personal preferences and aims: so that "loving Thee above all things we may obtain Thy promises."

What are those promises, in your case? That God, through His Spirit, will teach you, use you and support you—more, work through you—accepting you as one of His tools, part of His teaching apparatus. This position may or may not turn out pleasant for you. A real tool is seldom asked whether it cares to be used for a particular job or not, or even whether it feels able to do the job or not. But unless you accept that situation with all that is implied in it, God is not going to accept you, use you, and pour into and through your hearts something of His creative and enlightening love. So great humility, loyalty, devotedness are to rule your life of prayer: helping you, as Elisabeth Leseur said, to "sanctify all intellectual work by giving it a supernatural intention," and keeping you in constant remembrance of your total dependence on God, and because of this His total claim on your powers and your possessions —even perhaps those spiritual possessions which you think essential to your life. Your vocation is a very exacting one, and sometimes spiritual emptiness and exhaustion may be part of the price you have to pay for fulfilling it. Hungry and thirsty, conscious of your ignorance and poverty, you must still feed and cherish those lambs to whom you are sent; and out of your own need still give what you can to other souls.

Think for a moment of the story of the Feeding of the Five Thousand. From one point of view, it has something to say to you about your vocation. There is the multitude, hungry in the wilderness, without bread: that lack of religion, of God, in the modern world, and in the children of that world, which teachers quickly come to realize. You, like the apostles, feel very troubled and compassionate about it. "What is to be done? These people have no food"—they are hungry for the Bread of Life. And sometimes, like St. Philip, you are inclined to give it up; and say that only organization on a very big scale can deal with the position. But Christ's immediate answer to all that is simply the demand to translate your vague pity and benevolence into an action that costs you something—costs, indeed, all you have got. "Give ye them to eat." There is no suggestion of miracle: He just tells us to see to it, forget ourselves, and give what we have. We look desperately round, and our resources seem very inadequate—those wretched little bun-loaves, and few small fishes, the total content of our spiritual provision basket—but such as they are, they must be given without reserve. And the result of that trustful giving was and still is, that those poor resources of ours are taken, lifted to heaven and blessed, and made more than adequate; and not only for those we want to feed, but in the end for ourselves too. When all were fed, when the job was done, they gathered up twelve baskets full; one basket for each Apostle. As you know, the word translated "basket" is the little satchel in which the travelling Jew carried enough food for one day's journey, not more. No waste, but no stinginess. God does not starve His staff: He always leaves them, if they follow His plan for them and give without reserve to His children, with enough food in hand for the day. Give without reserve, and you will gather up enough to fill your own lunch-basket; only of course you must take the trouble to do the gathering up. I am afraid you may think language of this kind very homely for so great a subject. But it is no more homely than the language of the Gospels must have seemed to those who read or heard them first.

So we have added another item to the list of essential dispositions which should govern your inner life. A self-oblivious generosity in spending yourself, your energy and your resources—giving without stint to those you teach, even those little resources which seemed barely enough for your own needs; humbly trusting that, given over to God's purpose, they will turn out adequate after all.

And next, coming down to the actual method of our religious life—and we must have a method here as elsewhere—I think the teacher above all others should always remain very faithful to that contemplation of the mysteries of our Lord's life, His methods and His Spirit, which St. Ignatius considered the best of all trainings in spirituality. Those who were destined to carry His teachings through the world were trained by just living with Him: and it still remains by far the best plan for those who continue their work. For only the humble and faithful friends of Christ, who learn His method by watching, and are willing to be used in His way as channels for the message of God to men, leaving out both self-depreciation and self-esteem, can really be trusted to teach or show others any truth about God. And this art can only be learned by re-entering the atmosphere of the New Testament, and looking steadily and humbly at the pattern there put before us. Then it is that we see, more and more, what searching lessons He has to teach us about the way His work must be done. We see Him moving easily and safely between the two extremes that always threaten every teacher—an easy shallow popularity on one hand and a difficult exclusive superiority on the other hand. Each gets what he needs, because He always thinks of them, not of His own doctrine and person, or the novelty and importance of His message.

Those called to be His pupil-teachers in the world to-day might think a little about this. Look at the beautiful absence of rigorism, the gentle, flexible, life-giving method which is yet never sentimental, vague or soft; and consider what humbleness, what reverence for our common human nature this involves in One who is and has the Truth of God. Wherever He comes, He brings the life-giving mystery of the Eternal; but He gives the mystery in and with the homeliness, weaving together both worlds. What a lesson for us! And especially for those of us who have a secret, arrogant craving for what we call "purely spiritual things." Here there is nothing abstract and highbrow: no overfeeding or over-straining of childish souls: above all, no hurry to enlighten at all costs everyone He can reach. What a great supernatural art that is; the quiet, humble patience, whether of those who teach or those who are being taught. Whichever class we think we are in, really we are all students under the quiet eye of God; and we need to learn the artist's pace—commonly so much more deliberate than our own—never hurrying, yet never waiting too long. We must often be content in our work as teachers to put on a good primary coat, and let it dry; in spite of our natural eagerness to get on with the picture before the inspiration fades. That only results in a sticky mess. Christ often seems content to give quite gently and simply one great revealing truth; and then leave grace to act, fertilize, bring forth. To give light and help and teaching with that easy selfless generosity, and not ask about results—leave it to God, and make no effort to finish one's own picture or harvest one's own corn—this asks for a great self-oblivion and humility of mind. But only thus will you really serve the purposes of God.

Look at the parable of the Sower; and remember

it is the Sower Himself who speaks. Anyone who cares for gardening, or is sensitive to the life of the fields, knows how near in sowing and planting we feel to the Mind of God; how we seem to enter His rhythm and share His creative joy, in a way appropriate to our humble state. And now see what it seems like in the eyes of the perfect Sower, the one Divine Teacher. He puts first all the wasted effort, and acknowledges quite frankly that it *is* wasted. And next, all the disappointing results—the things every teacher has against him, the poor and shallow soil, the competing interests, the hostile influences choking the development of the good seed. All this has to be reckoned with. The Sower goes forth without bitterness or reluctance, knowing all that, and slogs steadily on. The handful of successes come last, and even those are graded: some a hundredfold, some sixty, some thirty. A perfect response is very rare. We have to carry on under just the same conditions; half-hearted acceptance, shallow appreciation, dull resistance, rejection of all that is not easy and pleasant, and waste of the seed we know is good. Self-esteem, however efficient, sowing its own seed and looking for results, soon crumples under that test. If it is our great privilege to be allowed to help with the sowing, we had better get the conditions well into our minds; face reality, and with it the fact that we shall never make a good job of our vocation, or escape the pitfalls of disillusionment, impatience, fed-up-ness, without a steady appropriation of the strength of God and a constant forgetfulness of self and loving subordination to His Will.

For after all, the position to which you have been called is splendid but difficult. All teaching worthy of the name is a form of Charity, Divine Love;

general devotedness to God and His interests, and
for His sake, to all the children of God. In one way
or another, you are required to be pupil-teachers,
working for love. You must learn all the time, and
give all the time; freely you have received, freely
give. That is your Charter. Only do see to it that
you fulfil the condition in which you can receive.
The most up-to-date and efficient tap is useless
unless the Living Water can come through and does
come through. Never let yourselves think for one
minute that because God has given you many things
to do for Him, a large number of restless lambs to
watch over, a great many pressing routine jobs, a life
that is full up with duties and demands of a very
practical sort—that all this need separate you from
communion with Him. God is always coming to you
in the sacrament of the present moment. Meet and
receive Him then with gratitude in that sacrament;
however unexpected its outward form may be. You
can and should receive Him, in every sight and
sound, joy, pain, opportunity and sacrifice; and
receive Him, not merely for your own benefit and
happiness, but so that you can freely give. The very
object of your inner life is the creation and maintenance of a secret music which shall support and
sweeten all your acts and words; constantly bringing
the sound of God to those you teach, and so those
whom you teach to God.

There is no work, practical or intellectual, which
cannot be given the colour of the love of God; nor
on the other hand is there any real contemplation of
His Majesty which does not find expression in active
love. Remember that our earliest English mystic,
Richard Rolle, was above all else a *teacher* of religion.
He taught both faith and conduct, he never separated

them. And all his teaching came out of his inner life
of adoring worship, was coloured by, saturated with
that. He summed it all up in one phrase, which
perhaps might be a motto for us too: "My heart thou
hast bound in love of Thy Name, and now I cannot
but sing it."

X

EDUCATION AND THE SPIRIT OF WORSHIP[1]

WHEN I first knew that I was to have the great honour of delivering the second Winifred Mercier Memorial Lecture, it came at once to my mind that in this Memorial we do not only commemorate a single-hearted devotion to one great cause, and a remarkable individual achievement. What we chiefly remember with gratitude and admiration to-day is a great human personality; for whom even that creative work, those absorbing practical activities to which she gave her life, only had supreme importance because they arose from certain deeply held convictions, embodied in the true Platonic sense an ideal, and pointed beyond themselves.

Every person who takes a hand in education is, to that extent, an artist in human life. Miss Mercier was such an artist; inspired in all that she planned and accomplished by that which St. Gregory called "the Vision of the Principle": the living Reality behind all appearance. It is because of this that I have called my lecture "Education and the Spirit of Worship"; though perhaps "The Spirit of Worship in Education" would come nearer to that which I shall try to say.

We are happy in coming together this afternoon as a body of people who share the same fundamental

[1] The Winifred Mercier Memorial Lecture, given at White-lands College, Putney, November 1937.

188

convictions about life. We are all members of the Christian Church; and so have a common faith and a common sense of obligation. We stand for the Christian view of human personality and therefore for Christian ideals of education. That is the first thing which matters about us. From the Christian point of view and in spite of all appearances to the contrary, every child that comes into our hands is potentially an inheritor of the Kingdom of Heaven and a member of the Communion of Saints. In the rough and tumble, the pressure of modern life, we have to remember that. Therefore Christian truth and Christian conduct—in other words, the Christian doctrine of God and of man—must form the ground-plan of the teaching by which you try to prepare the children in your charge for life. You see them, and the world in which they must grow up, from a parti-cular point of view; a point of view which is not that of the rationalist or of the materialist, or even of the humanitarian. As they must come to you as the creatures—more, the children—of God, committed to you by God, and endowed with spiritual possibili-ties, so the way in which you deal with them, the way in which you put the very facts that you try to teach them, will be conditioned by your own attitude to God; for this affects everything else.

You will perhaps expect me to talk about the way in which the teacher can develop the spirit of worship in her pupils. But I do not want to say very much about that. Indeed, there is not much that can profitably be said about it; for the spirit of worship cannot be expressed in a formula, or produced by suitable exercises. It is, as they say, "more easily caught than taught." What I do want to talk about is this: the fact that the ultimate value of the teacher to educate in the true sense of the word depends on the extent in which he or she possesses the spirit of worship—the habit of looking up and out beyond the frontiers of the useful and the obvious, and finding beyond those frontiers a beloved Reality which gives significance to the useful and the obvious. I am not now thinking only, or indeed chiefly, of what is called religious education. For the Christian, all real education is and must be religious from end to end. It must be filled with that deep reverence for life which alone enables us to interpret life.

Now the very object of education is to interpret life to the child: to bring some order into the confused mass of objects and experiences which besiege the awakening consciousness, and so put the growing human creature more and more fully in touch with the world in which it finds itself. The ultimate aim is gradually to set up a full, true relation between pupil and environment; and for Christians, the ultimate fact about that environment is, that it is the work of God, indwelt by God, and a means of serving, knowing and glorifying God. You remember how Angela of Foligno tells us in her *Book of Visions* that the Holy Spirit said to her, "*Look*, and see." Few people look, most of them only glance: but looking is the first step to worship. When Angela looked, she "saw that the whole world was full of God." That is a vision of which every real teacher must at least have a glimpse. All other facts about the world are subsidiary to it; and unless they are related to this primary truth, they merely bewilder us. This is true on every level of life: the levels we call physical, intellectual and social, no less than the level which, without knowing very much about it, we dare to call spiritual.

Therefore, every genuine teacher, and above all the Christian teacher, must at all costs get away, and keep away, from the corroding notion that imparting information is her main task; and I think we all know that this is not nearly so easy as it sounds. On one hand, introducing your pupils into life, more life, a wider, richer universe, and on the other hand, helping each to become a truly living personality—that is, or should be your main task. These two points—interpreting the world, and developing personality—cover, I think, the whole field of real education. The various subjects which you teach are subtractions from this total reality; the living and mysterious self which you are training, and its response to the living and mysterious world which you are revealing. These subjects, which we think so real and important, have little value in themselves unless they open doors and windows upon the whole; and interpret to the child, in a way it can understand, the strange mixed universe that surrounds it, and in which it can so easily get lost. They should, directly or indirectly, wake up and develop its aptitudes and powers, its wonder, its interest, its initiative—build up its sense of responsibility—make it fully human, fully alive. Your business is so to deal with the material given to you that it shall do this.

What has the spirit of worship to do with such a view of education? I think it has a great deal. For it seems to me that the fundamental question at the present time is really this: Which is education going to be—God-centred, and so, conscious of mystery, coloured by worship, essentially objective, humble, disinterested; or, man-centred, conscious of human claims and opportunities, and poised on material progress, self-expression, the exploitation of the world in the interests of men? The education of the future, as I see it, must take one of these two paths. It will concentrate on the useful, the this-world, the concrete, will accept a man-centred culture with the dreadful cheapness and flatness that goes with it— that hard, utilitarian form of humanism which is really a disguised animalism, since it leaves out the human spirit and its powers and deepest cravings— or else it will stand firmly for the Vision of the Principle, for a God-centred culture; a culture which does justice to the noblest longings and deepest intuitions of mankind, which looks beyond the here-and-now, relates Time and Eternity. A culture, in fact, which is informed by the Spirit of Worship, even though it may never use that term; and in that spirit seeks to interpret life.

The Christian choice between these extremes is obvious. This does not mean that Christian education, Christian culture, must be overtly pious, or look timidly at new methods, movements and discoveries; but it does mean that all these must and will be placed within the context of Eternity. It means that all is controlled by the opening words of the Office of Lauds—"The Lord is high above all people: and his glory above the heavens"—by that sense of a living Perfection, beyond and above anything that we can conceive, which irradiates the New Testament. You remember the passage in the Revelations of Julian of Norwich, in which she describes how there was shown to her in one of her visions a little thing "about the size of a hazel nut"; and it was said to her, "this is all thing that is made." That is the proportion in which for Christian thought the visible world stands to the spiritual world. And she saw in this little thing three properties; three things that mattered about it. The first was that God made it, the second that He keeps it, the third that He loves it. But what this Infinite Creator and Supporter and Lover might be, over against whose reality the whole universe was such a tiny thing—that was a mystery, in the presence of which she was silent. The teacher who sees the world in this proportion, as a small thing set within the great horizon of Eternity, held and cherished by an unseen Power, will give almost unconsciously—in and through the most practical subjects—a reading of life, and an introduction to life, which has, through and through, the quality of worship.

What is worship? It is the adoring acknowledgment of all that lies beyond us—the glory that fills heaven and earth. It is the response that conscious beings make to their Creator, to the Eternal Reality from which they come forth; to God, however they may think of Him or recognize Him, and whether He be realized through religion, through nature, through history, through science, art, or human life and character. These, of course, are the immediate subject-matter of education. How entirely different will be the outlook and the work of the teacher who places them in the context of the Transcendent—who does not first consider their here-and-now value, the contribution they make to successful living; but finds in them intimations of reality, hints of the Absolute —from that of the teacher for whom they are in themselves educational objectives. But it is only by entering into the mood of worship that we learn to realize this eternal and unchanging Truth and Beauty penetrating the historical and ever-changing order in which we live, and giving to it all its wonder and its significance. Everything becomes transfigured for

N

those who have achieved this point of view; who enter on the day's work in the spirit of the *Te Deum*, possessed by a total attitude of awestruck love towards the living mystery of Reality. "All the earth doth worship thee!" Physics and geography, zoology, botany, chemistry, geology—yes, even psychology, human wisdom's youngest and most unruly child—all swept into the single act of adoration, the response of the created order to the Divine Mind.

I said that the teacher's vocation has two parts. First, the teacher introduces the child into life, interprets the world to it. Secondly, there is committed to the teacher a creative task; the moulding and developing of personality. Consider how the spirit of worship will condition these two sides of your work.

First, the world into which you introduce your pupils will be, roughly speaking, the world which you are able to apprehend. Merely passing on text-book information about the physical universe does not cover your responsibility here. Unless you have developed in yourself the instinct for the beauty, the sacredness, the deep meaning of nature, you will never make anyone else feel this. But we cannot know anything as it really is, unless we have learnt to look at it with self-forgetful reverence, with admiration—in fact, with the eyes of worship— seeing it, not for our own sake, not mainly interested in its usefulness, but for its own sake, as an independent creature of God, existing for Him and to Him in its own right. "Contemplation," said our earliest English mystic, "is a loving sight," and there is a contemplative element in all real worship. It is those who see the universe thus, with disinterested adoring delight, who discover and are able to communicate its real secrets; for these secrets are only revealed to the eyes of love. That is a principle which can animate—or perhaps a better word is irradiate—the simplest, most elementary forms of education; and reveal the sacred character of the world that we live in, its wonder and its beauty, to the youngest child.

A pupil of that very great educator, Mother Janet Stuart, said in later life that one of the memories which had never left her was of an illness which she had whilst at school. During that illness, Mother Stuart came to see her every day, always bringing with her a few flowers. She only brought one of each kind, and about each she had something beautiful to reveal and interesting to say. But what the child remembered most vividly was the reverence and gentleness, the delighted love with which her visitor touched the flowers: that gave to her, as no words could ever have done, a sense of the wonder and holiness of living things. Janet Stuart disliked intensely the type of nature study which involves the pulling of living plants to pieces. She always preferred to teach by the patient study of growing things, never by the dissection of dead things; for then, she felt, it was difficult to preserve that which was far more important than any mere giving of information—the sense of the beauty and sacred character of all life.

In that small reminiscence we have, I think, the key to a complete educational programme, based on a particular attitude towards existence. It is a programme which, bit by bit, introduces the pupil into a larger, richer universe; where the humble beauties that surround us are given their rightful place, where our small problems and interests are seen in their right proportion, and where more and more we become aware of those spiritual realities which condition our true lives.

The gap between those spiritual realities and our apparent situation—between the great vision of the Principle and the teacher's everyday task—generally seems so great that only a steady feeling of the spirit of worship, a habit of delighted and humble adoration of the Perfect, a sturdy spiritual realism, can maintain our contact with the invisible Reality. Often a teacher may have to spend years in surroundings that seem to be almost devoid of spiritual suggestion. Yet this constant habit of looking beyond appearance towards the unseen perfection will help her to realize that here, too, everything is material to her great purpose; and can be interpreted in the light of faith, and woven into the life of worship. Unresponsive children, an unelastic system, the academic blight which lies on so much education still—all these different kinds of resistance will stimulate and not depress, in so far as she is able to look beyond them to the creative goal.

A traveller, who lately paid her first visit to Iona, was asked by the old Scottish gardener on her return to the mainland where she had been. When she told him, he said, "Ah! Iona is a very thin place!" She asked him what he meant by a thin place, and he answered, "There's very little between Iona and the Lord!"

I am far from denying that from our human point of view, some places are a great deal thinner than others: but to the eyes of worship, the whole of the visible world, even its most unlikely patches, is rather thin. It has a peculiar quality and radiance which attentive eyes can discover, and which comes from that which it transmits. You know how you may pick up a piece of stuff which is doubtless very useful, but looks dull, opaque, even grubby in the hand, and hang it in a window where the sun shines through. Then it is irradiated, glorified; discloses wholly unexpected colour. That is something like the difference between the world seen by those for whom it is a thin place, and the same world seen merely in economic regard, by those who never look beyond its relation to the problems and possibilities of everyday life.

To see the world in that sort of way is an essential part of the Christian outlook; for the Christian is committed to an equal belief in the reality of eternity and the reality of time. In the days that are coming, I am sure that Christianity will have to move out from the churches and chapels—or rather, spread out, far beyond the devotional focus of its life—and justify itself as a complete philosophy of existence; beautifying and enriching all levels of being, physical, social and mental as well as spiritual, telling the truth about God and man, and casting its transfiguring radiance on the whole of that world in which man has to live. It must, in fact, have the courage to apply its own inherent sacramentalism, without limitation, to the whole mixed experience of humanity; and in the light of this interpretation show men the way out of their confusions, miseries and sins. Only those who have learned to look at existence with a constant remembrance of the Eternal, with the disinterested loving gaze, the objective, unpossessive delight of worship—who do see the stuff of common life with the light shining through it—will be able to do that.

"I will lift up mine eyes to the hills"—not because geology is a set subject—not because I see signs that the flora may be rich and interesting—not because there may be opportunities for successful mining operations—not even because the air is pure and bracing and does me such a lot of good: but in a spirit of humble contemplation, delighting in the solemn beauty, the independent reality of that which lies beyond myself. It is not, of course, at all easy to do this and keep on doing it, in the pressure of a full and organized career. We can only manage it if we are fully persuaded of its absolute importance, of the fact that it is central to our vocation. But it *is* central, for we find in the long run that those who starve their capacity for worship, for admiring love, starve their real teaching power at its source; and therefore risk starving their pupils, just at that point where they most need to be fed.

Our interpretation of life always goes wrong when we focus our attention on one spot, and try to find in this the clue to all the rest. The eyes of worship have a wide-angle lens. They take in and resume a great stretch of experience, not only that which is immediately useful to man—nothing distorts reality so much as the utilitarian point of view—and in the light of this great vision they see human life, and interpret it, in a larger, nobler, more enduring way. In regard to education this, of course, matters supremely. All the separate bits of knowledge which you impart, the carefully fitted in tabloids of the time-table: knowledge of past history and present history, of the physical and mental worlds and the laws that appear to condition them—of language, number, measure, form and rhythm—in themselves, all these entrancing realities picked out from the rich flux of experience are only of secondary importance. What really matters about them is, that they contribute to the building up of an interpretation of life; that each is a partial manifestation of a greater whole, and is by that whole redeemed from pettiness. They need one all-embracing master principle to give them significance: and that principle can only be the creative Will of God.

It follows from this that those who see life with the eyes of worship are the only guides worth having to life. I will not say, the only safe guides. The young man from the tourist agency, with all the necessary information printed on little cards, and a reliable list of all the best hotels, is the safest of guides if we stick to his itinerary. But he will lead without enthusiasm on a well-worn track, show us all the usual objects of interest, take us to shops that sell nothing but souvenirs, and in the end we shall have seen—really seen—nothing at all. The overdriven teacher, once the first enthusiasm is past, lives under a constant temptation to take her pupils on a cheap personally conducted tour of that kind; eliminating risk and fatigue, taking all the short cuts, and covering as much ground as possible in the shortest possible time. To resist that temptation, fight that devil, is essential to her task. If you are really to lead your pupils to the mountains, it must be because you love the mountains; and every time you go there it is a fresh adventure, and you are ready for a fresh surprise. But you will never manage this unless you keep alive the spirit of worship. The spirit of worship is the very spirit of exploration. It has never finished discovering and adoring the ever-new perfections of that which it loves. "My beloved is like strange islands!" said St. John of the Cross in one of his great poems. Islands in an uncharted ocean, found by intrepid navigators after a long and difficult voyage, which has made great demands on faith, courage, perseverance. Islands which reveal beauties that we had never dreamed of, and a life of independent loveliness to which our dim everyday existence gives no clue: yet never reveal everything, always have some un-answered questions, keep their ultimate secret still.

This outlook upon existence, this astonished, awe-struck joy, which triumphs over all the anxieties, perplexities and sufferings of our common life, is an enduring, indeed an outstanding part of our Christian inheritance; far too easily neglected and obscured. It is of priceless value in building up a selfless and courageous temper of mind, releasing us from the stifling grasp of personal ambition and personal fear, setting our feet in a large room. That outlook trans-figures nearly every page of the Bible. It makes of the Psalms the greatest of all religious poetry; and it is the Psalms, more than anything else, which set the standard of worship for the Church. We find it, in its most rapturous expression, in the early liturgies; in those wonderful outbursts of adoration which seem as it were to lift us right up and away from the world of use and wont, and remind us of the other world pressing in.

"Who is sufficient to utter the wonders of thy power, or to show forth all thy praises? For neither could all living creatures, if they spoke with one mouth and tongue, be sufficient to tell of thy great-ness, O my Lord! For before thee stand a thousand thousand, and ten thousand times ten thousand angels and archangels, who all with one accord fly, and hover, and cease not to praise thee. . . . And with those heavenly hosts we also O gracious Lord, O Lord the Merciful Father, even we cry out and say, Holy art thou, and glorious art thou in truth and lofty art thou and exalted above all, who hast made thy worshippers upon earth worthy to become like those that glorify thee in heaven."

There is here an intensity of spiritual realism, a note of passionate joy, a real delight in God, which shames our timid this-world acts of worship. It asks for nothing. It does not want to improve anything, to learn anything; it is not concerned with what religion does for us, with what the old divines used to call the "profit of godliness." It is content to adore God in forgetfulness of self. Put beside this act of adoration, which comes to us from the very beginnings of Christianity, the same kind of vision as it came to a great religious poet of the last century, Gerard Manley Hopkins:

> The world is charged with the grandeur of God:
> It will flame out, like shining from shook foil . . .

And then consider, that it is this world "charged with the grandeur of God" which you are privileged to show to those you teach. Finally, look at the intimate, adoring response which a very modern writer—Walter de la Mare—who would perhaps hardly consent to call himself a religious poet at all, makes to that same splendour in his exquisite poem, "The Scribe":

> What lovely things
> Thy hand hath made:
> The smooth-plumed bird
> In its emerald shade.

And all the long list of the delicate beauties of creation. And then, the conclusion: the poet, by a tarn in the hills, reviewing

> Earth's wonders,
> Its live, willed things—

To find in the end,

> Leviathan told
>   And the honey-fly . . .
> My worn reeds broken,
>   The dark tarn dry,
> All words forgotten—
>   Thou, Lord, and I.

All three so different; yet inspired by an identical certitude, an identical passion for the sacred beauty lying behind life. Poetry is a great revealer of reality, a great incentive to worship; for it nourishes the sense of wonder, perpetually breaks through the hard crust of practical life, and lets in the other-worldly light. I am sure that the side of religion which most closely approaches poetry, which cannot be expressed at all without the use of poetry, is of the greatest importance for the Christian educationist, and especially perhaps at the present time; for the utilitarian spirit, which has gained such a dreadful ascendancy in modern education, has even infected much modern religion.

In a recent report of one of H.M. Inspectors on a school which had sought to brighten up morning prayers by introducing a little Scripture teaching, the Inspector said in conclusion, and with obvious approval, "Daily prayers at this school are now something more than a mere act of worship!" Even though few may go to these lengths, we all know that such questions as: "What is the use of religion?" "Does Christianity work?" "How is the Church going to help *me*?" "What do *we* get out of public worship?" are asked again and again in absolute good faith, especially perhaps by young people, with no consciousness of their essentially irreligious character.

No branch of the Church is really exempt from this tendency. We hear corporate worship, prayer, the sacraments again and again recommended on self-interested grounds, because they help us, do us good: or even because they are justified by psychology. Yet this utilitarian, ca' canny, self-interested piety is the negation of the spirit of worship; and tends to the production of self-centred, mingy little souls.

That is no ideal for the artist in human life. The Christian educator must make better use than this of the living, plastic material confided to her care. Her business is to help the growth of generous, noble, self-giving spirits; not centred on man and his opportunities, needs, problems, devices, but on God and His splendour and call. Only an attitude which is implicitly that of worship is likely to have any success here: an attitude which puts the practical and the profitable in its place, and keeps it in its place, but beyond and above this sees the spiritual, and its entirely non-practical call and demand. The breaking of the jar of precious ointment, which might have been sold for quite a good price—the giving of a life that might have been most successful—the sacrifice of an attractive career, a good position, and the quiet acceptance of something else—it is here that human nature rises to its heights; and it is for you to prepare your pupils for the realization of this. But you will only be able to show it to them in so far as you possess it yourselves. There is a passage in St. Paul's letter to the Philippians in which he says, looking forward to the possibility—indeed virtual certainty—of his own martyrdom, that it will be joy to him, if he is poured out as a drink-offering, a libation, on "the sacrifice and service of their faith." The drink-offering, of course, was the most wasteful, useless kind of sacrifice that could be imagined from the practical point of view. Some sacrifices did provide food for the priest or the offerer; but this was poured out, soaked into the ground, and lost. That "sacrifice and service of faith," which the Philippians were already offering—good, solid, practical Christianity —had obvious merits and uses, which anyone could appreciate. But the drink-offering, like the jar of precious ointment, was giving just for giving's sake; an act of pure and self-oblivious worship. Yet it was the idea that he might be asked for this which delighted St. Paul, and seemed to him the crown of his career.

Thus we arrive at the second, and supremely important and crucial point, at which the spirit of worship will radically affect the teacher's outlook, and therefore the way in which she does her work. We have seen that it can, or will, entirely transform the way in which she looks at the world which she is called to interpret. How will it affect her attitude to the children themselves? Surely it must transfigure her whole relation to them; for it will mean a realization that a bit of this living, growing universe on which she looks with such reverence and delight, has been given to her to deal with: as regards each child in her care she is, as St. Paul said, a fellow-worker with God. She has been taken into the workshop. For Christianity is not a series of beliefs; it is a creative religion. Its object is to make new creatures; and a bit of this creative work is given to every teacher. Though she may never realize it, each of these plastic and growing human spirits will be different because of its contact with her. This means that its response to life, its effect on other human spirits, will be different. We cannot estimate the final effect of the relation between the teacher and each child, for it stretches out to eternity and is lost to our sight. That is rather a sobering thought; yet also an exhilarating thought. It brings into the foreground your creative responsibility. The whole child stands before you as a little creature of God, on whom He desires to work through you.

A great deal of stress is laid now on this fact of the child, as the primary reality for the teacher. Child Guidance, Child Psychology, are subjects of outstanding importance which, rightly used, help her to do her work in the best possible way. But unless this technical study of the child nature is coloured through and through by a deep and humble sense of the sacred and mysterious character of the material with which the teacher is privileged to deal—if it produces a doctrinaire habit of mind—if she gets lost in psychological detail and jargon, and loses sight of the beauty and mystery of the living thing—above all, if her aim is only to produce healthy and efficient little citizens, well balanced and well informed (though, of course, this, as far as it goes, is a Christian task), then her great creative opportunity will have been missed.

I said that the teacher is admitted to the workshop and becomes a fellow-worker with God. In the workshop, a good deal of drudgery is involved in the first shaping of the raw material, and this raw material does not show much sign of that which it is going to become. In fact, at that stage, it often looks very unpromising. Many a young teacher, entering on her career with high hopes and ideals, has been badly disillusioned by contact with the actual child. Yet it is a fact, all appearances notwithstanding, that each one of those children is a child of God and a member of Christ. The seed of supernatural life has been planted in it. It has its part to play in the mystery of Incarnation and Redemption. It is a candidate for eternity. Her recognition of that profound fact, and because of that recognition the way in which she handles the half-made thing—always as it were tending to slip through her fingers, and never reacting in quite the way she expects—will be very important for the finished result. To put it in another way, the teacher's place is in the pond among the wriggling tadpoles; and at that stage it is hard to realize what the frog will be like, with its wonderful adjustment to two levels of life, in water and on land. Of one thing we can be sure. Though the creative action of God on human personality is free, and He can work the most amazing transformations of the most unlikely material—restless, narrow, hard, self-centred souls—still, in a general way, there will be a direct connection between the quality of the developed frog-life and the quality of its tadpole stage. The dignity of the teacher's profession, one of the greatest of all professions, is that it demands of her the effort to produce that quality: to make each tadpole a first-class tadpole, physically, mentally and spiritually. She will never do that unless she keeps the frog in mind; for no creative work is well done by us unless we remember the relation between the very small part we are able to accomplish and the finished product and its place in the total plan. That means that the teacher, working in the world of time, the tadpole world, and limited by that world of time, must never lose her sense of the Eternal—that vision of the Principle with which we began—must be devoted to its interests, believe in it, trust it and love it, and because of this, believe in, trust and love every life committed to her care.

See then how greatly your work must depend, and through that work the children of the future must depend, on Faith, Hope and Charity. And Faith, Hope and Charity are the essential attributes of the spirit of worship; for worship means a total and selfless devotion to the great purposes of creation—believing in those purposes, trusting them, caring for them, more than we care for our own interests. It means, not lovely feelings—which always fail us at a pinch—but an austere dedication of the will; which, because it is so utterly disinterested, kills the self-centred fears and anxieties of our generation at their root. Those whose privilege it is to educate the children of the future can hardly do them a better service than inducing in them this sturdy, selfless, yet exacting attitude towards life.